NEGOTIATING
Constructive and Competitive Negotiations

Bill Scott

Incorporating contributions from Ian Morley, David Sutton
and John Winkler

PARADIGM PUBLISHING
1988

Paradigm Publishing
Avenue House
131 Holland Park Avenue
London W11 4UT

© Bill Scott, 1988

Set by Anneset, Weston-super-Mare, Avon.

Printed in Great Britain by
St Edmundsbury Press Ltd, Bury St Edmunds, Suffolk

First published 1988

British Library Cataloguing in Publication Data
Scott, Bill, *1925–*
   Negotiating : constructive and competitive negotiation
   1. Management. Negotiation
   I. Title
   658.4'5

   ISBN 0-948825-26-X

Dedication: Deb

Contents

PART 2   COMPETITIVE NEGOTIATION

Note to reader

PURPOSE

This book is drafted as a textbook for the use of business and management students and for lecturers on business-orientated courses.

SCOPE

This book is concerned with commercial and allied negotiations.

The processes in this book are directly applicable to the technical discussions which precede many major negotiations and to the allied discussions on finance, services, and legal aspects.

Since points and examples may be offered more easily in the commercial mould, the majority of examples are taken from that world.

The forms of any negotiations have degrees of similarity. The individual negotiating next year's salary will find it helpful. So will those involved in domestic negotiations.

The book throws incidental light on the subjects of Industrial Relations, political, government and hostage negotiations, but these are not the main thrust of the book.

The main thrust is towards commercial and allied negotiations.

ORIGINS

The origins of this book lie in my role as a consultant working internationally with highly experienced negotiators.

When first involved in this aspect of consultancy, I found myself working with people rich in experience, people handling massive deals. In common with many people of such quality, they were eager to see if they could develop their skills as negotiators.

At that time, it was not easy to find literature or other help which reflected the practical skills of such negotiators. There was ample literature from the world of theory, particularly the fields of mathematics and psychology. The academic excellence of this literature was not, however, reflected in its practical merit.

The more practical literature stemmed largely from American thinking. This reflected a style of negotiating performed effectively by American negotiators, a style well suited to the American character. It was not a character which was natural to negotiators from other countries, other cultures.

As I worked increasingly with such experienced negotiators and was able to learn more of the way in which they negotiated, I was able to develop some fresh practical thoughts. These were first published by Gower in *The Skills of Negotiating* (1981), a book which has earned the reputation of being the leading practical work in the field.

The present volume both up-dates and advances the thinking contained in that original book.

In addition, the book is enhanced by independent expert contributions.

ADDITIONAL CONTRIBUTORS

David Sutton, one of the country's leading case-study writers and external examiner for business courses, has contributed case material and exercises particularly appropriate to a student audience.

Ian Morley, of the University of Warwick, has added reading lists both for each chapter and for the book as a whole.

John Winkler, an independent consultant and one of the world's recognized authorities on marketing and on bargaining, has contributed a chapter on Price Bargaining.

THE ABILITY TO NEGOTIATE

The ability to negotiate is a skill. It is something to be developed and polished in the same way as the skill to swim or to ride a bicycle. It depends on experience and there is no substitute for experience.

Knowledge can be taught. Experience can be compressed in working seminars—I earn my living through conducting such seminars—but experience cannot be taught.

Knowledge becomes profitable—beyond the passing of exams—only when backed by experience. But at this time, there is no standard textbook which enables students to pick up the basic knowledge.

This book aims to fill that gap. It is about negotiating. It is for lecturers and students.

A NOTE ON LANGUAGE

In the absence of a generic third person pronoun in the English language, the word 'he' is, please, to be taken to mean 'he' or 'she'.

Bill Scott
21 Hartley Crescent
Southport

Foreword

This book will help you to learn the process of negotiation, but you need to consider carefully the practice of negotiating as much as the theory, and you will not negotiate successfully unless you practise.

For these reasons, each chapter of the book closes with a summary highlighting the main points and with exercises to help you to test your understanding and to develop the skills you need.

Please tackle these exercises. They will add immeasurably to the benefit you derive from reading the book.

D.F.S.

Acknowledgements

Stella Ascott, JP
Jeremy Swinfen Green
Lynn Harrington

About the Contributors

BILL SCOTT is a management consultant, specializing in the fields of negotiation and communications. He works in countries ranging from England to China, from Norway to Nepal and New Zealand.

His previous background includes a rich mixture of industrial and university experience. In his present role, he has won an enviable reputation for the conduct of effective and enjoyable seminars in his chosen fields.

He is author of *The Skills of Negotiating* (Gower 1981), *Communication for Professional Engineers* (Thomas Telford 1984), *The Art of Managing* (with Sven Soderberg) (Gower 1985), *The Skills of Communicating* (Gower 1986), *Constructive Negotiation* (Gower TFI 1986).

IAN MORLEY is Senior Lecturer in Psychology at the University of Warwick, and has been studying the skills of negotiation for almost twenty years. He is the author of one academic text, *The Social Psychology of Negotiation* (with G.M. Stephenson) and has written a large number of articles on the subject. His other academic interests include the study of leadership, group decision making, inter-group relations, and engineering design.

DAVID SUTTON is experienced as an examiner in business studies and as an external examiner.

He has fifteen years' experience as a member of the DMS panel of the CNAA. As such, he has great experience of the needs for sustaining standards in management education.

His previous experience is strong in both industrial and academic life. He is now an established and successful management consultant and his specialities include the field of negotiating.

JOHN WINKLER is internationally renowned for his seminars in negotiation and pricing techniques which have been held in more than twenty countries.

Previously marketing director for Buxted Chickens and J. Lyons, John Winkler knows the negotiation environment well. A former marketing correspondent of *The Times*, John Winkler has been running seminars from his offices in Brighton since 1969. His companies produce a variety of training material from computer programs through to training videos and personally led, specifically designed seminars.

CHAPTER 1
Types of Negotiation

INTRODUCTION

The purpose of this opening chapter is to establish the shape of the book you are starting to read.

Let us begin by looking at some examples of people negotiating.

EXAMPLES

Martin McLean is a trainee buyer. He has an appointment to receive Guy Smithson.

Guy arrives at his office. Martin shakes hands and sits down behind his desk. Guy, seated on the other side of the desk, reaches into his briefcase for his papers.

"Well now," says Martin. "Thank you for coming. What's your price for these widgets?"

"Our widgets are performance tested and guaranteed," says Guy. "Let me tell you about the way they are made."

"That's all right—I don't need to know the details of how they are made, but I do need to know the price. What is your price?"

In this example, the two people are heading quickly towards a point at which they are likely to disagree.

Martin is concerned dominantly with price. He is of a mood to get an offer then to show his mettle by trimming it down.

Guy sees it coming. He tries to slip in the defensive machinery, the plus points for his product, but from the outset he is on the defensive. He is, inevitably, beginning an aggressive defence.

From the outset, they are heading for controversy.

Charles Blackman is another buyer. His appointment is to receive David Stanton.

After suitable greetings Charles and David settle down to business.

Charles opens. "Well now, I shall be interested to hear what you can tell me about your ability to supply widgets. Should I first tell you our situation?"

"That would be most helpful. I will be delighted to tell you all I can, but I would be better informed if you would give me some idea of your requirement."

"Right, then. Let me say at the outset that we know of your reputation. We know of you as a new company entering into this field. We have heard reports about your vigour and drive and innovation. Frankly, we don't have any direct evidence of your performance and we don't have evidence about your deliveries or your service . . . We are always anxious to ensure that we deal with up-and-coming people and I am much looking forward to hearing what you have to tell me.

"Our immediate need is for . . ."

Here we find a very different approach. Charles and David are both seeking to exchange information. Each sees a need to get information from the other. Each is not only prepared but even anxious to offer information to his counterpart.

Ellen Jones, Charles Blackman's technical colleague, visited Mats Jonsson, her technical opposite number in Scandinavia.

They had a long discussion in which Ellen stated a specification of what they were looking for. Mats told her how closely they could manage to meet that specification. They then negotiated the closest specification to their joint requirements.

Charles became involved in the commercial discussions with the same prospective suppliers.

The deal involved complicated arrangements to finance and to guarantee the costs of the deal. Charles set up meetings between his financial director, Ernest Tomkins, with his bank manager in attendance, to meet the Scandinavian finance director and their export credit guarantee board.

All of the above negotiations are within the scope of this book. All are concerned with commercial and allied negotiations.

The following are examples of different types of negotiation, on which this book will throw only incidental light.

The newspaper headlines described the negotiations between the Employers Federation and the Trade Union. The Trade Union had put in a claim for 15 per cent, the Employers Confederation have responded with an offer of 2.7 per cent. The paper's industrial correspondent speculated on the characters of Alf Smith (the Trade Union's General Secretary) and on George Carpenter (the Employers Confederation representative) and on their abilities to outwit one another. News reporters contributed rank-and-file views. An editorial in the centre pages talked about the present state of industrial relations.

This is a negotiation carried out under the glare of publicity. The protagonists are referred to as antagonists from opposite sides. The issues under negotiation are identified only in the starkest items: the rates of pay, the hours of work, the length of holidays. There is no reportage of the softer items which may be more important: loyalties, goodwill, mutual respect, diligence, work satisfaction.

The parties are seen to be in dispute. Constructive movements are reported as concessions, compromises, surrenders or victories.

Whatever the basic attitudes of the parties to the negotiation and to one another, they are publicly seen to be at loggerheads and publicly expected to justify the extreme positions they are reported to have taken.

For many years, Denis Healey and Sir Geoffrey Howe exchanged epithets with one another in public. Phrases such as "Hunting the familiar fleece of friends from the Foreign Office" and "Another lugubrious concentration of meaningless cliches".

When Denis Healey retired to the back benches, he and Sir Geoffrey Howe were seen on television as robustly convivial colleagues who had shared intimate discussions in private at the same time that they were heard publicly to be in raucous conflict.

This is negotiating in politics. The real business is set up through friendly but tough negotiations, hopefully after long and careful preparation. The reported processes may well be a façade for that reality.

An aircraft is hijacked. A negotiator has the task of securing the release of the passengers and, indeed, of the aircraft.

A businessman or reporter is taken hostage in Lebanon. Somebody— Terry Waite is an outstanding example—seeks to negotiate with their captors.

These are examples of hostage negotiations.

Three students agree to share a flat. They have to reach agreements on how they deal with electricity bills, bathtimes, housework, telephone.

That's negotiating one's private affairs.

CONSTRUCTIVE AND COMPETITIVE NEGOTIATIONS

This book is about commercial and allied negotiations.

Such negotiations may be carried out in different ways and this book will highlight the distinction between two different styles.

Consider again the second Example: Charles and David settled down to business together.

They were Constructive Negotiators.

Please read again the first Example: Martin and Guy, from the outset,

3

acted in ways which were likely to goad one another.

They were acting as Competitive Negotiators.

The book which you are starting to read has three main parts.

Part 1 describes **constructive** negotiation.

Part 2 focuses on **competitive** negotiation.

The two final chapters are of interest for both styles.

SUMMARY

1. This book is concerned with commercial negotiation.
2. It is not primarily concerned with other types of negotiation: IR, political, hostage, personal, etc.
3. Commercial negotiations can be conducted constructively or competitively.
4. This book will first tackle Constructive Negotiations and then come to Competitive Negotiations in Part 2.

EXERCISES

1. What are the key differences between constructive and competitive negotiating styles?
2. Which style of negotiation would you personally prefer to conduct? What does this tell you about your own personality?

FURTHER READING

Walton, R.E. & McKersie, R.B. (1965) *A Behavioral Theory of Labor Negotiations*. New York: McGraw-Hill.

This is the classic text on collective bargaining. Walton and McKersie identify four sub-processes. Distributive bargaining is based on perceptions of difference between the parties. Integrative bargaining is based on perceptions of common problems and complementary interest. Attitudinal structuring functions to modify or maintain relationships developed during the process of bargaining. Intra-organizational bargaining is bargaining between negotiators and the groups they represent. If Walton and McKersie are correct the interaction between the sub-processes means that negotiators face a variety of dilemmas in negotiations. These are examined in detail. The book contains many examples of actual negotiations, and frequent reference is made to interviews with professional negotiators.

Further discussion of Walton and McKersie's work is given in:

Morley, I.E. (1981) *Bargaining and Negotiation*. In Cooper, C.L. (ed.) *Psychology and Management: A Text for Managers and Trade Unionists*. London: The British Psychological Society and Macmillan Press.

Anthony, P.D. (1977) *The Conduct of Industrial Relations*. London: Institute of Personnel Management.

Warr, P. (1973) *Psychology and Collective Bargaining*. London: Hutchinson.
An introductory text written around a case study of a pay and productivity agreement. Emphasizes the similarities between negotiation groups and other decision-making groups.

Strauss, A. (1978) *Negotiations: Varieties, Contexts, and Social Order*. San Francisco: Jossey-Bass.
This book is divided into two parts. The first provides a critique of existing models of negotiation. The second provides case studies of negotiation designed "to illustrate the very considerable range of different negotiation processes" (p. 97).

Marsh, P.D.V. (1984) *Contract Negotiation Handbook*. Aldershot: Gower Press (2nd edn).
Deals explicitly with commercial rather than industrial relations negotiation. Some of the book is rather technical in nature. However, the analysis is informed by the author's practical experience in negotiation, gained for example as a Director of Wimpey International Limited.

Video Arts (1985) *So You Think You Can Sell?* London: Methuen.
This is the book that goes with the training films. One chapter is explicitly devoted to negotiations between buyer and seller. The authors include John Cleese, Jonathon Lynn and Anthony Jay.

McCall, J.B. & Warrington, M.B. (1984) *Marketing by Agreement: A Cross-Cultural Approach to Business Negotiations*. Chichester: Wiley.
Presents a mode of negotiating skill derived from work on stages in negotiation. The model is used to analyse sales/purchase negotiations in a variety of countries.

Lockhart, C. (1979) *Bargaining in International Conflicts*. New York: Columbia University Press.
An excellent and very well written treatment of political negotiations, describing the bargaining which occurs in severe international conflicts.

Baldwin, J. & McConville, M. (1977) *Negotiated Justice: Pressures to Plead Guilty*. London: Martin Robertson.
Describes some aspects of plea bargaining in the Birmingham Crown Court.

Heumann, M. (1978) *Plea Bargaining: The Experience of Prosecutors, Judges and Defense Attorneys*. Chicago: University of Chicago Press.
Describes plea bargaining in American Circuit and Superior Courts.

Miron, M.S. & Goldstein, A.P. (1979) *Hostage*. New York: Pergamon Press.
Miron and Goldstein present case studies of hostage negotiations, such as those involved in the kidnapping of Patricia Hearst. They show how lessons from the cases have been used to guide the training given to the New York State Police, as part of their Counter Terrorism and Hostage Program.

Filley, A.C. (1975) *Interpersonal Conflict Resolution*. Glenview, Ill.: Scott, Foresman.
Provides a number of useful examples of negotiating one's private affairs.

Scott, W.P. (1981) *The Skills of Negotiating*. Aldershot: Gower.
Presents a preliminary treatment of the skills of constructive and competitive negotiation. Much of the material complements what is written in the present book.

PART 1
CONSTRUCTIVE NEGOTIATION

INTRODUCTION TO PART 1: CONSTRUCTIVE NEGOTIATION

At the outset, we need to set the scene.

We must first of all look at the context of *constructive* negotiations. What is distinctive about the context? (Chapter 2).

Then, before we can look at technique, we need some way to analyse a negotiation, some framework. (Chapter 3).

CHAPTER 2

The Context of a Constructive Negotiation

INTRODUCTION

This chapter sets the context of a constructive negotiation.

Within the more general context of any negotiation we will consider the values, attitudes and behaviour in a constructive negotiation.

CONTEXT

The representatives of two organizations are meeting.

They may be assumed to be people of the same status. That is, neither will have a directing role such as that held by the chairman of a meeting, or by an interviewer at a selection interview. There are certain niceties which the host may be expected to perform, offer tea or coffee, ensuring adequate seating and so on. But the host is not normally expected to dominate the way in which the negotiation is tackled.

The parties will normally meet in private. Either party may bring in external advisers, but all present will be expected to respect the confidentiality of the negotiating room. They will not be subject to the scrutiny of public gaze.

Each party must operate within a range of constraints. There are legal constraints and precedents. At the end of the negotiation, the parties may have settled on a deal and in so doing arrive at a commitment to one another.

That is the context of any negotiation in private.

There are three distinctive features about the context of a **constructive** negotiation. These features are largely bound up in the **values** which the negotiators bring to the meeting.

1. They are concerned to create the most significant level of deal. They are not necessarily restricted simply to the item which was top of the agenda as they first met.
2. They want to move towards agreement. They do not expect to create dissent.

3. They seek mutual advantage. They do not want simply to benefit at the expense of the Other Party.

ATTITUDES AND BEHAVIOUR

Arising from those basic values, the constructive negotiator brings distinctive attitudes to the negotiating table.

He esteems the worth of the Other Party. The person with whom he is negotiating is to be respected as a professional.

He is a man whom it is important to be able to trust. Not to be trusted absolutely of course—none of us can be trusted absolutely—but one whom we would wish to trust if he earns the benefit of our inevitable doubt.

This other person with whom we want to do business (or continue to do business) and to build foundations for continuing business and benefit in the future.

The constructive negotiator seeks to establish creative possibilities. He looks to build the maximum deal from which both parties may benefit to their joint satisfaction.

He recognizes that there are bound to be differences between the interests of the two parties. He seeks to reconcile those differences to their mutual advantage.

Those are parts of his attitudes.

If he is to play his part and to earn the trust of the Other Party, then his behaviour must reflect those attitudes.

He must be honest.

He must be reasonably open, prepared to offer frank statements about his interests, about what he can offer, and about what he hopes to achieve.

"Reasonably open": he must be prepared to tell the truth, openly. There will be some point at which he may be reluctant to tell the whole truth, but it must nevertheless be the truth.

His behaviour must at all times reflect his values of looking for long-term possibilities, working towards agreement and seeking for mutual advantage.

EXAMPLES

In the examples which we use through this book, a number of characters will reappear. The characters in constructive negotiations may be commercial people, or they may be technical, financial or other experts. Engineers, bankers, lawyers, many technical specialists. For ease of description, we shall mainly use commercial examples: buyers and sellers.

1.	Martin McLean Guy Smithson	Martin and Guy are respectively buyer and seller. They are in two different companies. They will move from one company to another but will remain buyer and seller. They are bright young men, but so far have little experience of the business world. Each is keen to make his mark in that world.
2.	Tina Thorne Sara Brady	Tina (buyer) and Sara (seller) have both built several years of business experience. They have each found themselves negotiating and have come to the conclusion that they would like to develop the skills of negotiating constructively.
3.	Charles Blackman David Stanton	Respectively buyer and seller, these are wily old birds who have been negotiating for a long time.
4.	Lew Daniels Howard Lacy	Lew and Howard will become more frequent visitors when we come to the world of competitive negotiating. Each is well experienced in that style.
5.	Ellen Jones Ernest Tomkins	Ellen is a technical expert and Ernest a financial expert. Each carries through his/her negotiations with opposite numbers in other companies and each occasionally becomes involved in commercial negotiations.

Let us consider some characteristic comments of these characters.

1.	Martin:	"Let's start at the important point. What's your price?" And having heard the price: "Oh, that's very much more than we can afford. You will have to improve on that."

Martin is anxious to show his mettle. His first consideration—his only consideration at this stage—is to get the best possible price.
His characteristic comments are provocative.

2.	Tina:	"Thank you for telling me what you are able to supply. Can you please now tell me your terms and conditions?

11

"Thank you for that explanation of terms and conditions. I must say at the outset that the price is beyond our means."

Tina has sought harder to create a constructive negotiation and has moved a great deal of the way along that path. Still, when it comes to the critical moment of discussing price, she focuses so hard on that issue that it will be difficult to avoid a fight with Sara.

3. Charles:

"Thank you for that explanation of your possibilities and of your terms and conditions. I have already briefed you about our specifications. Looking at the commercial issues, our priorities are price and quality. We are, of course, concerned with best position on the other terms and conditions, but there is quite a gap for us to bridge on price and on quality: and those really are our priorities. Can we talk about how to bridge the gap?"

Charles does not have to think about this sort of issue. He knows that there are ways of wording things which enable people to be constructive, and he automatically uses those forms of words.

He would have handled the early stages much as Sara but now, as the critical price discussion approaches, he does not isolate it as something to be fought over. He wraps it in a range of variables. He invites his opposite number to regard differences as gaps to be bridged. Together.

4. Ellen:

"Thank you for that information. If I have got it right, you could match us on tensile strength or on shear but you could not manage both at the same time.

"I think that for us the tensile is the more important. If we were to stick to specification on that, what would be the effect on shear?"

Ellen is investigating. She will aim to use this discussion to reach the optimum balance in joint interests. That's constructive.

5. Ernest

"The difference then is that you would wish us to take 60 per cent of the capital cost and then give us 40 per cent on deferred terms. Our offer is the other way around—40 per cent plus 60 per cent.

That means we must overcome a difference

of 20 per cent on the capital account. How would you feel about our throwing the problem to our respective bankers and telling them to sort it out?"

Ernest looks for ways to overcome differences, rather than force concessions from his opposite number. Equally constructive.

SUMMARY

1. The context is a meeting of two organizations in private with possibilities of doing a deal.
2. The constructive negotiator values:
   (a) Creating the most significant deal.
   (b) Searching for agreement.
   (c) Seeking mutual advantage.
3. His attitudes incline to:
   (a) Esteem the worth of the Other Party.
   (b) See him as a prospective business partner and friend.
   (c) Search for creative possibilities.
   (d) See differences as gaps to be bridged.
4. His behaviour is honest and reasonably open, seeking to gain the trust of the Other Party.
5. In practice, he is careful to avoid a fight.

EXERCISES

1. When negotiating a new contract for transporting the College football team to away matches, which features under discussion would you use as a basis for finding points of agreement?
2. What areas would you expect to show the biggest differences in approach between firms quoting for the contract?

FURTHER READING

Walton, R.E. & McKersie, R.B. (1965) *A Behavioral Theory of Labor Negotiations.* New York: McGraw-Hill.
What Walton and McKersie call integrative bargaining is one clear case of constructive negotiation. It is often treated (mistakenly) as if it were the only case.

Pruitt, D.C. (1981) *Negotiation Behavior.* New York: Academic Press.
Discusses the forms taken by integrative agreements and outlines some of the processes which may be involved. The text relies very heavily on the results of laboratory research using games of conflict, or role playing tasks.

Fisher, R. & Ury, W. (1983) *Getting to Yes: Negotiating Agreement Without Giving In*. London: Hutchinson.
Argues that competitive negotiations are difficult, dissatisfying and frequently do not work. The book describes a method of constructive negotiation, developed at the Harvard Negotiation Project in the United States. The tactics described have special force in legal contexts. Nevertheless, the book is one of the best how-to-do-it texts on the market today. Special attention is given to the point that negotiators have many interests in the negotiation and will judge success or failure in many ways. This is so important that Fisher and Ury advise negotiators to reconcile interests rather than compromise positions. Those who would like a more detailed, academic treatment of this theme will find excellent value in:

Gulliver, P.H. (1979) *Disputes and Negotiations: A Cross Cultural Perspective*. New York: Academic Press.
This is one of the best theoretical treatments of the process of negotiation. However, it is very clearly an advanced academic text.

de Bono, E. (1985) *Conflicts: A Better Way to Resolve Them*. London: Harrap.
Introduces the idea that solutions are better designed with the help of third parties than negotiated directly by the participants in a conflict. However, many of the tactics introduced by the third parties could be used by the negotiators themselves.

Strauss, A. (1978) *Negotiations: Varieties, Contexts, and Social Order*. San Francisco: Jossey-Bass.
Strauss divides negotiations into those which are competitive and those which are cooperative. He provides a detailed case study of the negotiations which led to close economic links between the Benelux countries: Belgium, the Netherlands, and Luxembourg. These negotiations involved many issues and were extremely complex. They were constructive in Bill Scott's sense.

Morley, I.E. (1987) Negotiating and Bargaining. In Hargie, O. (ed.) *A Handbook of Communication Skills*. London: Croom Helm.
Introduces two important ideas. The first is that negotiations have to solve cognitive problems (they need to organize their intellectual activity, and learn to think clearly about the issues) and political problems (differences between the parties generated by differences in goals or by differences in basic outlooks). Evidence is summarized which shows that skilful negotiators remove unnecessary obstacles to agreement. However, they are not afraid to disagree. They recognize, better than less skilful negotiators, that some kinds of compromise are worse than useless in the long run. The second idea is that negotiations cycle through competitive phases, which differentiate the positions of the parties, and collaborative phases, which integrate the positions of the parties. It seems that skilled negotiators are able rapidly to switch between competitive styles, in which they function as 'intergroup antagonists', and collaborative styles, in which they function as group problem-solvers.

Karrass, G. (1985) *Negotiate to Close*. London: Fontana.
   The idea that constructive negotiators help those on the other side of the table
   is taken up in Karrass' book. Karrass also gives examples of many other facets
   of constructive negotiation.

Fisher, R. (1971) *Basic Negotiating Strategy: International Conflict for
   Beginners*. London: Penguin.
   Do not be put off by the title. Although Fisher deals with international conflict
   he introduces some quite general ideas for making negotiations constructive,
   and getting something practical accomplished. Fisher's book is very clearly
   written with some very thought-provoking examples.

Filley, A.C. (1975) *Interpersonal Conflict Resolution*. Glenview, Illinois: Scott,
   Foresman.
   Reviews research which identifies different personal styles of bargaining, and
   the attitudes which support them. A great deal of attention is given to methods
   of integrative decision making.

CHAPTER 3
A Framework for Negotiation

INTRODUCTION

The process of negotiating is complicated.

We sit there thinking about widgets. The quality problems we have been having, the difficulties we are having with cost and delivery, and the batch which Buggins is sending back claiming it is too late. The mess up on the accounts going to another customer. The heat in this room as we sit at this negotiating table. The way the other chap is looking at us, and the problems of meeting his demands while still making a profit. The fact that we have already been here for 3 days and it looks like going on for another 2. And what about the other clients we should have been seeing tomorrow?

There is such a mass of impressions and thoughts pressing on us, each related in some way to the other, yet all very imprecise and blurred.

However blurred and grey the picture may be, we have to put it into black and white terms before we can discuss it and gain control of it.

We need it simple.

This chapter is to provide a simple framework for considering and eventually controlling negotiations.

FRAMEWORK

In any negotiation we are concerned with subject matter. That is, the technical area in which we have expertise. If we are bankers, it is banking. If we are engineers, it is engineering. If we are widgetmakers, it is widgets.

The negotiation of that *subject matter* depends on a number of foundations.

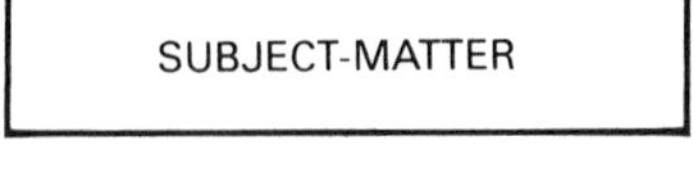

> SUBJECT-MATTER

Fig. 3.1

We can think of those foundations as being on three levels (Fig. 3.2).

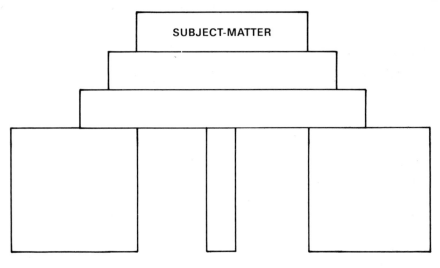

Fig. 3.2

At one level, we discuss the subject matter in some sort of sequence. The conversation breaks up into a series of successive points. One or other of us talks first . . . longer or shorter . . . changes the subject . . . summarises.

What we talk about, who talks, how long, even why. These are matters which determine how our negotiation will develop. These we include in the *procedural* foundation for our discussion of the subject matter.

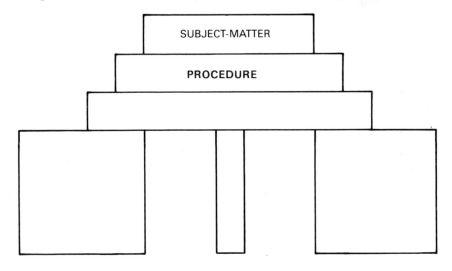

Fig. 3.3

17

Then there is the "people" level of foundation. We are influenced by the man sitting opposite us. How far can we trust him? Is he a helpful sort of person? Is he the sort of person we want to work with? Or should we be constantly on the defensive?

These are all aspects of the *climate* which pervades the discussion.

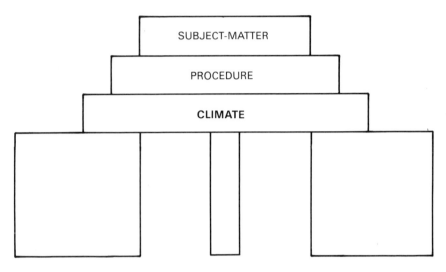

Fig. 3.4

Throughout our negotiation we have to be conscious of the way that the procedure is developing and of the climate that is developing as well as handling the problems of our widgets. Our minds are very heavily loaded—often overloaded.

In order to establish control—of ourselves and of the negotiator—we must get our thinking into order.

Think now of our negotiation as taking place over a period of time. In the diagram which we are developing, time is along the axis from left to right.

At the bottom level of our foundations there is, in advance, the way we organize our thinking.

Our *preparation*.

And after the negotiation, setting the scene for our future success in later negotiations, there is the effectiveness with which we *follow up* (Fig. 3.5).

EXAMPLES

When Guy called to see Martin about the possible supply of some widgets he found himself ushered into the office and very quickly, he was making a presentation about the widgets. A skilful presentation, well rehearsed and well illustrated.

Guy received a lot of interested questions from Martin and managed to give him plenty of information. He was a little startled when Martin's secretary came in to say that the next visitor was waiting. Nevertheless, he quickly wrapped up his presentation.

He went away regretting that he had not managed to make a deal, and feeling that fate had cheated him.

Guy did not establish the climate at the outset of the negotiation.

Nor did he check on procedure. He was astonished, for example, to discover that Martin had another visitor so quickly.

He had not laid the opening foundations.

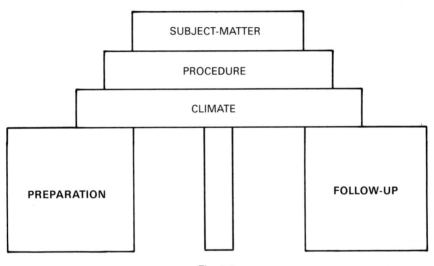

Fig. 3.5

Later in the day, Sara went to see Martin. She took a couple of minutes at the outset talking about his office and decorations.

As they sat down she enquired how much time Martin could spare, and then suggested that she would like a briefing about his needs, and equally would like her chance to present her own products.

Sara got off to an altogether better start.

Analysis
Guy had prepared a professional presentation but the way in which his meeting developed was like Topsy. It just grew.

Thus Guy was caught off-balance when the secretary interrupted. He was not in control of time.

Nor did he establish a suitable climate. Guy might as well have been talking to an impersonal robot as to a human being.

Sara, on the other hand, established a more personal climate from the outset and soon had a sense of plan and of pacing (time) for her meeting.

She put effort into establishing both the procedure and the climate for the negotiation.

Moreover, there was a difference between the forms of preparation which each had done.

Guy had polished his skilful presentation.

Sara had thought about presentation and had also thought about Martin's likely interests. She knew she needed to know more about them.

And she had thought more about the procedure she would want to follow.

She had prepared differently in advance. She sought to establish appropriate foundations of climate and procedure from the outset.

CRITICAL MOMENTS

To be in control of a negotiation, we must have considered all of the framework through which it will evolve.

As it evolves there are going to be some critical moments. Moments of particular significance when what happens in a short while, has a disparate influence on what will take place afterwards.

There will inevitably be critical moments which we cannot anticipate. We will have to react to them there and then.

But there will always be some critical moments which we can predict.

The greater our ability to predict critical moments, to plan for them and to control them as they arise, the greater our ability to be in control of the negotiating process.

Two of the critical moments can be predicted as a matter of time.

The first is at the outset. When people meet, their first impressions are critical. These first impressions are of lasting significance. In particular, the climate of the negotiation becomes fixed (Fig. 3.6).

And the way their expectations are influenced in these opening moments creates a lasting impression for the whole of the negotiation.

Soon, the discussion moves into areas which are important but not critical.

As time goes by, the discussion may even be taken up by items which are not particularly significant (Fig. 3.7).

Through these middle phases there will be some critical moments, but the general trend will be to items of lower significance. Less than the critical opening moments.

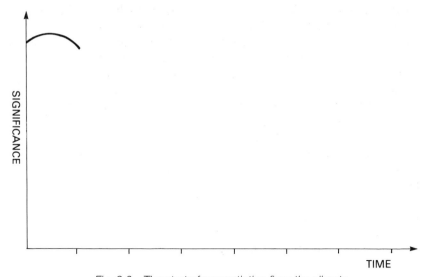

Fig. 3.6   The start of a negotiation fixes the climate

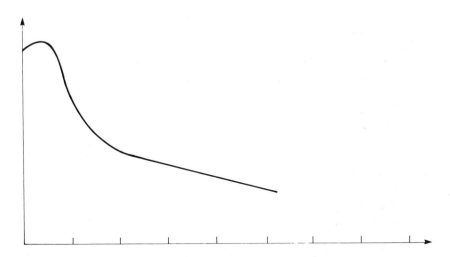

Fig. 3.7   As negotiations continue discussion moves into less important areas

This movement of course will not be continuous. The trend will be downwards but there will be some moments of richer importance within the trend (Fig. 3.8).

Some of the variations on the trend can be predicted and we will be discussing them in later chapters. It is within the power of the negotiators to vary the timing of those critical points.

21

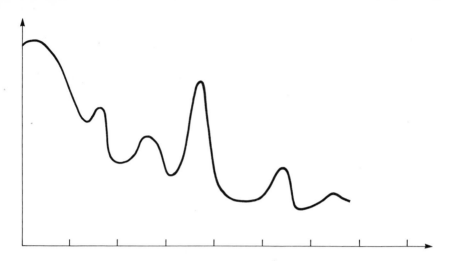

Fig. 3.8   Throughout a negotiation there will be moments of richer importance

It is not within their power to vary the timing of one other critical point. This is the final phase of the negotiation. In a relatively short burst of activity at the end of any negotiation (Fig. 3.9), matters of great significance can be agreed. They contrast with long-winded discussions which have taken place in the preceding period.

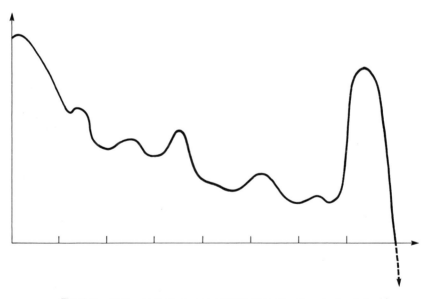

Fig. 3.9   At the end of any negotiation there is a burst of activity

SUMMARY

1. Negotiating is a complicated process. We must reduce it to simplicity if we are to tackle it practically.
2. In this book, we shall use a simple framework in which the subject matter rests on three levels of foundation:
   (a) The procedure which we adopt
   (b) The climate of the negotiation
   (c) The preparation beforehand and the follow-up afterwards.
3. There are critical moments in any negotiation.
4. Always, the first act and the last act are of critical importance.

EXERCISES

1. As President of the Students' Union you have to negotiate for the re-decoration of the bar. You are to meet the bosses of three small firms of painters and decorators who have put in highly competitive quotations. How would you establish the most desirable atmosphere for these meetings?
2. What areas of differences and difficulties would you anticipate in the forthcoming negotiations? How would you plan to deal with them?

FURTHER READING

Morley, I.E. (1981) Bargaining and Negotiation. In Cooper, C.L. (ed.) *Psychology for Management: A text for Managers and Trade Unionists.* London: The British Psychological Society and Macmillan Press.
Argues that to study negotiation at all we shall have to simplify what is going on. Sets out five models which are simple to use and help to identify the skills negotiators need. What is needed is a description of the process of negotiation which is sufficiently simple to act as a guide to action, and sufficiently complex to be practical. That is to say, we should be looking for ideas which are simple but powerful. Those readers who would like to see what a more complex model would look like are referred to:

Druckman, D. (ed.) (1977) *Negotiations: Social Psychological Perspectives.* Beverly Hills, Ca. Sage.
Druckman, D. (1977) Human Factors in International Negotiations: Social Psychological Aspects of International Conflict. *Sage Professional Papers in International Studies* **02**(020). Beverly Hills: Sage.

Video Arts (1985) *So You Think You Can Sell?* London: Methuen.
Describes constructive negotiations between buyer and seller in terms of ten simple rules. The rules are justified by reference to a two-person negotiation about a contract for ten motorway machines.

Kotter, J. (1981) *The General Managers*. New York: The Free Press.
This book is not about negotiating, although negotiating will be part of a general manager's job. Kotter shows quite decisively that the more effective managers had a much clearer picture of what they were doing, and why they were doing it.

Torrington, D. (1982) *Face-to-Face in Management*. Englewood Cliffs, N.J.: Prentice-Hall.
Derek Torrington has written a series of books based on the assumption that managers' social skills will be improved if they use a simple structured approach to a variety of encounters. His book contains chapters dealing with negotiation and arbitration. However, the organization of the chapters reflects only the lowest level of Bill Scott's three foundations.

Miron, S. & Goldstein, A.P. (1979) *Hostage*. New York: Pergamon Press.
Shows the importance of adopting a systematic approach to hostage negotiation. Many of the themes have a more general application.

Rubin, J.Z. (ed.) (1981) *Dynamics of Third Party Intervention: Kissinger in the Middle East*. New York: Praeger.
The importance of the three levels introduced by Bill Scott is shown very clearly in some treatments of third party roles, particularly Rubin's introduction.

What negotiators do before they meet, is extremely important. But let us first look at what happens when they meet before we consider what they need to do in advance of that meeting.

We shall be concentrating on constructive negotiation, and will first consider levels 2 and 3 in the framework: that is, the foundations of climate and some aspects of procedure.

Then we will analyse and discuss technique in handling the subject-matter.

All this before we get into the areas of preparation, tactics, control.

The sequence of the next chapters on constructive negotiation will thus be:

(a)   The climate of a constructive negotiation: What it needs to be and how it is formed (Chapter 4).

(b)   The opening processes (Chapter 5).

(c)   The subject matter of a negotiation: The structure of a negotiation (Chapter 6). The opening phase of a constructive negotiation (Chapter 7). Later phases (Chapter 8).

CHAPTER 4

The Climate of a Constructive Negotiation

INTRODUCTION

The first topic for discussion—the first foundation—is the climate for the negotiation.

In this chapter we shall consider the situation in which the climate becomes formed then the sort of climate we want.

We will follow up with some examples and suggestions about behaviour.

SITUATION

The parties to a negotiation are meeting, having in mind the possibility that they will do business together.

They are aiming to create a constructive negotiation.

Each comes to the meeting room with his mind full of recent experiences. The visitor has come from his travel, from any work which he has been doing on those travels and from the hassle of the airport, the railway or the car journey. The host has been in his office dealing with office business. Probably dealing with colleagues insisting on their own priorities and with the everyday problems confronting any executive. The negotiators come from different backgrounds. Unless (most unlikely) both of them have taken the time to compose their minds as they arrive, they will not be on the same wavelength.

Yet they are entering a critical period in the negotiation. A period during which important and durable impressions will be formed, influencing the course of the whole negotiation.

It may be a meeting between old friends. In that case, it is relatively easy to find a common wavelength and to discuss common interests.

Often, it will be a meeting between people meeting for the first time and inevitably establishing some chemistry between them. Positive or negative.

The climate for negotiations is formed very quickly. Each of us has the experience of meeting new people and of very quickly forming a judgement about whether these are people we want to go on meeting.

It is true of the student meeting other students, the student meeting his tutor, the student meeting a prospective landlady to discuss (negotiate) taking rooms.

Very quickly, each of us forms some lasting impression of that other person. It was equally true when Mrs. Thatcher met Mr. Gorbachev. It was a short meeting, long before the latter became the Russian leader. From a relatively short meeting, Mrs. Thatcher emerged saying: "He is a man I could do business with".

At the outset of a meeting then, people come together and quickly form important views about one another—views which will condition the way they try to do business.

What sort of climate should they try to form? A desirable climate.

Here are suggestions for the sort of climate we should seek to establish for a *constructive* negotiation.

Natural. Many businessmen like to have a friendly and reasonably relaxed manner in negotiations. For them, that is a natural characteristic of a meeting.

But there are some times when they meet other people with different views. Beaurocrats and Germans, for example, adopt a formal attitude in negotiations.

It is no use trying to impose one's own characteristic on people who would be uncomfortable operating that way. Subject to that reservation, "be natural".

Here are four other characteristics for the climate:

Cordial. A polite, sympathetic and almost friendly atmosphere.

Co-operative. Parties working together towards an agreement in their mutual interests.

Brisk. Moving at a measured pace towards a settlement. Neither wasting time nor rushing it.

Businesslike. Focusing on the key matters of importance to the Parties.

EXAMPLES

Martin was seated behind his desk as Guy opened the door. He looked up, pushed aside the papers he had been reading and said:

"Good afternoon."

Guy walked towards him rather slowly—he did not want to seem overpowering to the man behind the desk and he was a little embarrassed.

"Er, good afternoon, er . . ."

With his jacket over his left arm and his briefcase in his right hand, Guy was a bit at sixes and sevens. He had to park his case on the floor,

27

then at last he could reach out to shake hands with Martin.

"Yes, well, er, you've come to talk about the widgets . . .," said Guy as they sat down.

No serious attempt, and no competence, in establishing a good first foundation. Hesitant, stumbling pace already established.

But suppose they got far enough to justify a later meeting . . .

Approaching another meeting a couple of months later, Guy had not been looking forward to seeing Martin again. He had been worrying about Martin's demands concerning quality during their previous meeting, and he walked into the office warily.

Martin, rising to meet him, sensed this mood.

Martin: "Good afternoon. How have things been going with you?"

Guy: "Pretty well. Sorry about the problems last time. I hope we manage to get round them all right."

Martin: "Well, of course there were difficulties and I hope you've been able to improve on the quality."

Martin's first question at least opened the way for Guy to develop some cordial remarks. But straightaway, Guy was into business and almost at once, they were heading for difficulties. Once again, they were not off to a start which was either cordial or co-operative.

As David approached Charles Blackman's office, he took a couple of deep breaths and switched his case to his left hand.

He entered the office to find Charles rising from his chair and, walking smoothly towards Charles, they met and shook hands as David reached the corner of the desk.

"Charles, good to see you."

"Hello, David. Good to see you too. Hope you had a good journey?"

They were already talking in a confident and relaxed manner.

"Yes, fine, thank you. And I find those new visitors' parking spaces a great help."

"Glad about that. Can I take your coat? And how's the fishing? What sort of things are you doing at this season of the year?"

Confident and relaxed. Positive pace established. David and Charles are already setting up the cordial tones.

SUGGESTIONS

The pace at which people move to meet and greet one another may be slow, hesitant, or at the opposite extreme, thrusting and overbearing. Somewhere between those extremes, each of us sets some sort of speed by the way in which we walk and talk. Within seconds, the potential briskness of the meeting is being established.

The next characteristic is the cordial character. Too quick an approach to business issues leads us too quickly towards areas of personal conflict. It is easier to open on neutral ground: the journey, the weather, the sports programmes, holidays, hobbies . . . .

The setting for this opening contact is also important. If one sits down opposite somebody else, eyeball to eyeball, it is difficult to establish cordial relations. It is easier to establish them when the parties stand and when the parties are not eyeball to eyeball.

Most people find it helpful if they can get focus onto something both can see. A picture on the wall. A bit of sculpture. The view from the window. Anything where the two can stand *together* and look at it *together*.

Sara and Tina. "Good morning. Nice to be here. Oh, is that a new painting over there?"

They immediately find themselves standing TOGETHER looking at IT. Much easier than head-on, and there's plenty of small talk begging for attention. The colour, the painter, personal preferences.

And so at the outset of the negotiation, the parties have come together and within a brief time, have taken steps which should establish the pace and the cordial nature of the meeting.

It may be a brief time, but it's so important to get it right. My rule-of-thumb is to think of five per cent of the meeting time being taken in this ice-breaking. If it's going to be a one hour meeting, use three minutes for it. If it's going to be a couple of weeks, have dinner together the previous evening. Keep off business. And when you meet again the following morning, again take two or three minutes.

We have yet to establish the businesslike and the co-operative dimensions: we will be turning to these in the next chapter. But before leaving this chapter, let us make a few suggestions about sustaining the climate in the later stages of a negotiation, and about the setting.

The climate will modulate as the negotiations develop. Inevitably, it will be influenced by growing agreement (or disagreement) on the subject matter. Not only by what is being said, but also by what the others are reading into what is said. That is inevitable.

The climate can, however, be helped by taking a few simple steps.

For example, take reasonably organized breaks. A toilet break every hour and ten minutes around the block *together* every couple of hours.

A cup of tea or coffee.

A smile works wonders. And the two parties finding a common cause to laugh about is even better.

The setting has an influence on the climate.

Fig. 4.1   Seating arrangements which cause a face-to-face confrontation can result in a less cordial and co-operative climate

If you seat visitors opposite the window—especially if opposite a sunny window—they will be, at the least, discomforted. Whether you do it accidentally or deliberately, they will wonder about your motives and may suspect that it's a ploy to make them uncomfortable and less effective. You'll be doing damage to the climate.

If you arrange the seating so that you are in the face-to-face confrontation, your setting is less cordial and less co-operative than it needs to be. If you have a square table for two people conducting a negotiation, then sitting adjacent to one another gives a better climate than sitting opposite (Figs. 4.1 and 4.2).

SUMMARY

1. As people meet, some chemistry quickly becomes established between them.
2. The suggested climate for a constructive negotiation has these characteristics:
   Natural
   Cordial
   Co-operative
   Brisk
   Businesslike

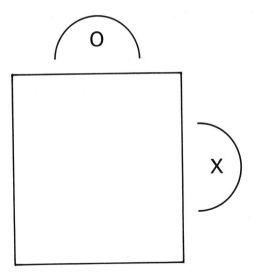

Fig. 4.2   Adjacent seating around a square table gives a better negotiating climate than sitting opposite

3. The prospective pace of the meeting is indicated by the way in which the parties walk and talk as they first greet one another.
4. There is merit in establishing a cordial climate before starting into possible controversial issues.
5. The suggested means is to concentrate on neutral topics, standing, and focusing on some object which can be seen and discussed.
6. As the negotiation develops, take occasional breaks from business, take light refreshments together, and try to develop a smile or a laugh together.

We have discussed the sort of characteristics we want in the climate and suggested ways to establish the brisk and cordial character. We have yet to establish the co-operative and the businesslike dimensions.

EXERCISES
1. Prior to, and at the commencement of, a negotiating meeting what steps would you take to establish a positive climate?
2. What factors will you take into account when deciding on your opening remarks?
3. How would you respond to an overtly hostile opening from the other party to a negotiation?
4. Construct four different arrangements for the seating of two teams at a negotiation, assuming you have two teams each of three members

and a rectangular table. What are the advantages and disadvantages of each?

FURTHER READING

Saunders, C. (1987) Opening and Closing. In Hargie, O. (ed.) *A Handbook of Communication Skills*. London: Croom Helm.
Begins with the statement that "First encounters in all human relationships are crucially important". Summarizes the literature on the social skills of opening and closing conversations of various kinds.

Zajonc, R. (1980) Feeling and Thinking: Preferences Need No Inferences. *American Psychologist*, **35**: 151–175.
This is a paper from a well-known academic journal. The title is well chosen since the main point of the paper is to show just how quickly evaluative judgements are made on the basis of non-verbal cues. Zajonc also points out that the non-verbal behaviour of other people may be a response to something we have done, rather than an indication of their own state of mind.

Argyle, M. (1978) *The Psychology of Interpersonal Behaviour*. Harmondsworth: Penguin.
Michael Argyle has done more than anyone else in the UK to analyse the nature of non-verbal communication. His work, and that of his associates, suggests that unsatisfactory social relationships are often the result of unsatisfactory social skills. They are not necessarily the result of enduring emotional or motivational problems. Argyle has also suggested some of the ways in which a variety of non-verbal factors combine to express attitudes of hostility versus friendliness, or dominance versus submission. This is a very useful introductory text.

Rozelle, R.M., Druckman, D. & Baxter, J.C. (1987) Nonverbal Communication. In Hargie, O. (ed.) *A Handbook of Communication Skills*. London: Croom Helm.
This chapter provides a detailed and up-to-date review of research findings. It summarizes what has been learned about non-verbal behaviour as a communication skill, using examples from studies of the police, selection interviews, interviews between doctors and patients, and corporate executives. The chapter is not for the beginner, but provides a very useful source of references for the interested reader.

Miron, M.S. & Goldstein, A. (1979) *Hostage*. New York: Pergamon Press.
Contains a very interesting section on building rapport. It is also very important to appear businesslike and to show that you know what you are doing.

Karrass, G.W. (1985) *Negotiate to Close*. London: Fontana.
Karrass' book says a great deal about the importance of climate, although climate is not mentioned in its own right. The short chapter on The Power of Wooing is particularly interesting.

Nierenberg, G.I. (1973) *Fundamentals of Negotiating*. New York: Hawthorn.
Contains a discussion of the characteristics of defensive and supportive climates.

Video Arts (1985) *So You Think You Can Sell?* London: Methuen.
Shows the importance of controlling the pace of a negotiation, and some of the dangers of premature agreement.

Filley, A.C. (1975) *Interpersonal Conflict Resolution*. Glenview, Ill: Scott, Foresman.
Very few texts on negotiation discuss the effects of variables such as seating arrangements and other aspects of climate. Filley's text outlines some introductory ideas.

Scott, W.P. (1981) *The Skills of Negotiating*. Aldershot: Gower.
Presents a short and very useful set of ideas on creating the climate of a constructive negotiation.

CHAPTER 5

Opening Procedure

INTRODUCTION

We have begun to build the climate foundation but need to take more steps to establish the co-operative and the businesslike character. At the same time we are anxious to move towards business.

In this chapter, we shall look at the situation we are in and at the suggested procedure. We shall follow with a couple of examples and some comments on them.

THE SITUATION

We have met and taken steps to get on the same wavelength socially. We need to move towards business without rushing too quickly into matters which will be controversial. Diagrammatically, we have met as two parties on different tracks (Fig. 5.1).

We have taken some small first steps towards eventually meeting in an agreement (Fig. 5.2).

We need now to start bending our paths a little further towards one another, continuing the movement from Figure 5.2 to Figure 5.3.

We need that extra fraction of movement.

We are still within the critical opening stage of the negotiation and we need to make the most of it. How can we do so?

One thing which bedevils any negotiation is ambiguity. Capable negotiators sitting down together can tackle and often resolve problems which they can identify together. Some competent negotiators are bemused when they feel things going on which they cannot understand. When the situation is ambiguous. It would help if we could reduce that ambiguity from the outset.

At this same opening stage, each party has come with some expectations about the meeting and some feeling about how it will unfold. Shared expectations, agreed expectations, are a strong link between the parties as the negotiation subsequently develops. Divergent expectations are creators of discord.

And at the same time, the co-operative and businesslike dimensions of

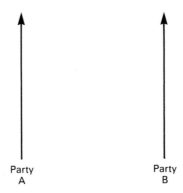

Fig. 5.1

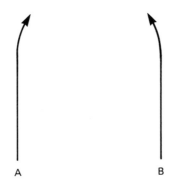

Fig. 5.2

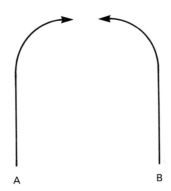

Fig. 5.3

the negotiation still need to be established.

There is now a possibility to reduce ambiguity, to create expectations, and to become co-operative and businesslike.

Suggested Procedure

First of all, we have to be careful. If the Other Party wants quickly to start on some pet subject, we have to be sensitive. If we try to deflect him from that topic, he can become resistant. Let's be responsive to his lead if we can.

But more positively, at the earliest opportunity, establish from the outset that we are people who can *agree*.

Agree on something semi-neutral. Something that helps us to move co-operatively towards increasingly serious business.

If you can introduce it, try to achieve agreement on the semi-neutral issue of procedure.

By "procedure" in this context, we mean *purpose, plan* and *pace*.

Agree the *purpose*, the reason why we have come together. If his purpose is different from yours, then be ready to compromise. Do, however, *agree* on a joint purpose for the meeting. Is it, for example, to be simply an exploratory meeting? Or is it to settle a deal? Or to ratify a deal previously agreed orally? Or to negotiate one particular detail of a larger deal? Or what? Why are we meeting?

Agree on a *plan*. An agenda. A sequence which the parties can follow together, without that cloying uncertainty which follows if both dash into a negotiation without any sense of direction.

Agree on a *pace*. Decide on the amount of time which both parties think would be reasonable and how tightly they need to keep to that schedule.

EXAMPLES

Martin and Guy—respectively buyer and seller—meet in Martin's office. The meeting focuses on Martin's interest in buying new paper supplies. Martin opens the meeting:

Martin: "Good morning. Thank you for coming. Now I am interested in supplies of copy paper. What is your price for copy paper?"

Guy: "It depends on the qualities. We can supply 45 gsm at £3.90 or 55 gsm at £4.50."

Martin: "Well, now, I was hoping that you could get a little below that . . ."

Tina and Sara also met to talk about paper supplies.

Tina took time to welcome Sara, to set her at ease and to offer a cup of coffee. As they sat down, Tina said:

Tina: "Well, I am pleased you are here. My concern today focuses on our suppliers of copy paper, and I would like to have an exploratory discussion with you. If you can give me some early thoughts, it might be that we would need to meet again in a couple of weeks' time to take matters a stage further. Would that be all right?"

Sara: "Yes, that sounds fine to me."

Tina: "I have set aside forty minutes for this meeting. Maybe we can move more quickly, or if necessary I can take a bit longer, but does forty minutes sound realistic to you?"

Sara: "I am at your service and that is entirely convenient to me. Have you any thoughts about how we tackle the discussion?"

Tina: "How would it be if I first told you a little about our requirements and then you can fill me in with the sort of things you can offer? Then we ought to be able to see in what ways we could try to set up some sort of deal."

Sara: "That sounds fine to me. I must say I would be most interested to hear about your requirements."

Comments

Martin and Guy rushed headlong at business and were quickly on to the most controversial issue. Neither had any idea of how the other expected the discussion to develop.

Tina and Sara, having broken the ice before they sat down:

    Agreed the purpose of the meeting

    Agreed a rough plan

    Agreed on timing

They emerged with:

    A procedure they could follow in a businesslike way

    An agreement to co-operate in the negotiation

    Having reduced the ambiguity about the way the negotiation might develop

    Having joint expectations of how it would develop and what end point they would try to reach

Tina and Sara were in a decidedly better position than were Martin and Guy.

This discussion of the opening procedure has assumed that the parties meet without having previously (for example in correspondence) agreed an agenda.

Even when such an agenda has been previously agreed, the parties arrive from their different backgrounds with that agenda at the back of their minds.

It boosts the prospects of the negotiation if they remind themselves at the outset that they are people who can and have agreed on something.

It boosts prospects even further if both can bring into their consciousness the agreed purpose, plan and pace. That the agenda they have agreed is . . . That their objectives and their times are . . .

This brief repetition reinforces the co-operative and businesslike start to the meeting, whilst reducing ambiguity and reconciling expectations.

SUMMARY

1. The parties sit down having, hopefully, established a cordial and brisk character for the meeting. They still need to establish the co-operative and businesslike dimensions.
2. They have the opportunity to bend their paths more towards one another before they get into controversial matters.
3. The suggested opening is to *agree* on procedure.
4. Aspects of procedure to be agreed are purpose, plan and pace.
5. Even when those aspects of procedure have been agreed prior to a meeting, it is helpful to bring them again to the front of people's consciousness.

EXERCISES

These questions all refer specifically to the negotiation for the redecoration of the Students' Union bar referred to at the end of Chapter 3.

1. Define in not more than twenty words the purpose of the meeting.
2. Would you enter into detailed negotiating at the first meeting or would you use it as an opportunity to narrow down the field to one firm with which to negotiate?
3. So far as you can, plan a procedure for the meeting(s).
4. How will you try to pace the meetings?

FURTHER READING

Bellow, G. & Moulton, B. (1981) *The Lawyering Process: Negotiation.* New York: Foundation Press.
    Bellow and Moulton argue that whilst the initial encounter establishes certain important parameters (cordiality, co-operativeness, etc.), the most critical job to be performed in the opening is to establish ground rules which make the

negotiation predictable. As they say, "Many of you may be 'thrown' by the unexpected in this stage of the process, often conveying more uncertainty, insecurity, and concession flexibility than you intend" (p. 135). Bill Scott's advice is designed to prevent this happening.

Warr, P. B. (1973) *Psychology and Collective Bargaining*. London: Hutchinson.
Warr gives a very useful case study which shows some of the difficulties which arise when management and union fail to agree on a plan and set an appropriate pace.

Video Arts (1984) *So You Think You Can Manage?* London: Methuen.
Much of what Bill Scott has said is the application to negotiation of ideas about management. The section "Meetings, Bloody Meetings" is especially relevant.

Scott, W.P. (1981) *The Skills of Negotiating*. Aldershot: Gower.
Argues that the very first moves in a negotiation do two important jobs. First, they set the tone, mood, and pace of a meeting. Second, they give clues about the characteristics of the other negotiators. They show something of his or her experience and skill. And they give clues to his or her style.

CHAPTER 6

The Structure of the Subject Matter

INTRODUCTION

Thus far, we have been looking at two of the foundations of a negotiation. We have covered the parts which are shaded in Figure 6-1, the climate and the opening procedure.

It is now time for us to move up into the subject matter.

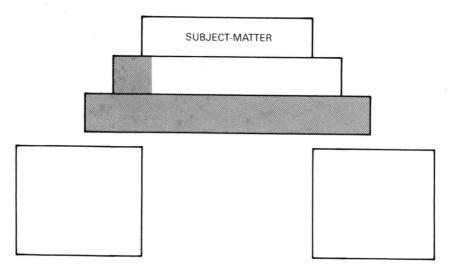

SUBJECT-MATTER

Fig. 6.1

THE NEED FOR STRUCTURE

Most negotiators make careful technical preparations for a negotiation. They then go off to a meeting formidably equipped to handle the technical discussions: specifications, the quality limits, the prices, the deliveries, whatever.

Often, they go to those negotiations with only hazy ideas about the way in which the discussion will evolve. Such negotiators pay penalties in five different ways:

1. The penalty of ambiguity. They are hazy about the way the discussion is unfolding, hazy about what line has to be covered, hazy about how this will be covered. During the negotiation, there is this constant background of uncertainty gnawing away at their ability to concentrate on the vital issues under discussion. They're in a haze. A bit bemused.
2. Not only are they hazy. They cannot control the direction which the negotiations are taking.
3. Their statements are ill-timed. Note, for example, the force of the comments about goodwill which appear in the examples below. Weak if at the wrong time. Powerful if at the right time.
4. Many negotiators miss the chance to make the most of "ripeness". There are some critical points of a negotiation which cause unnecessary difficulty if confronted before the time is ripe. For example, a price—mentioned only after both parties had seen the advantages of reaching a deal—might be accepted without comment. The same price, expressed at an earlier stage, might antagonize the Other Party. It is a question of ripeness.
5. The technique which a negotiator needs to use at one phase of a negotiation differs from the technique he should be using at another.

To take advantage of the opportunities of a negotiation, to avoid the pitfalls, the negotiation must fall into some sound structure. Here is the one we suggest:

The Structure of the Subject Matter
Take the box at the top of our negotiating framework:

Fig. 6.2

Divide it into four stages and label them as shown in Figure 6.3.

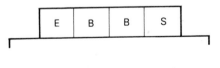

Fig. 6.3

The four initial letters stand for:
Exploration
Bidding
Bargaining
Settling

Exploration. A phase of finding out where one another stands, and whether interests can run together.

Bidding. Establishing what one or both parties want in terms of money and other variables.

Bargaining. A period of reconciling the differences between the parties.

Settling. The final move towards agreement.

Let us take up a couple of illustrations.

EXAMPLES

Imagine that two companies have agreed a contract for the supply of equipment worth £1,000,000.

Whilst the equipment is still at an early stage of being manufactured, the order is cancelled by the buyer.

This is a well-known commercial situation and is usually covered by a cancellation clause in the contract. But often, the urgency of business life is such that the supplier has to get moving quickly if he is to achieve delivery promises. He often has to proceed before such details as cancellation terms can be thrashed out.

Then in the event of cancellation, the buyer and the seller have to negotiate some settlement.

Martin:	"Good morning. Thank you for coming over to discuss this affair.
	"I am sorry about what has happened."
Guy:	"Yes, me too. It seems we have quite a problem."
Martin:	"Oh, well, I am sorry about that. But I don't suppose that you had got very far ahead with our order?"
Guy:	"Well, we had done all the planning, and we've had to have research experts involved as well."
Martin:	"Do you mean that there is a question of money involved? How much?"
Guy:	"Well, if you look at all those things and add them all together, and allow for the costs of disruption, in total it comes to £400,000."
Martin:	"What?! Forty per cent of the total cost? That's way outside

	anything I would have expected. How on earth do you justify that?"
Guy:	"Well, we have the costs we have incurred, we have the overheads, we have had to change the whole production line. We have had to invent work to keep our people going."
Martin:	"Even so, this is grossly excessive, and just think what it does to the goodwill between us."
Guy:	"On the contrary. It is perfectly reasonable . . ."

Martin and Guy skimped the establishment of Climate and Procedure and then almost totally omitted Exploration before coming to Bidding. They were immediately set on a damaging path.

Imagine Charles and David meeting under the same conditions. They would spend some time ice-breaking and re-establishing their business relationship and they would talk about how they intended to tackle the discussion. Suppose they agreed that David should start by presenting the situation as he sees it.

David:	"Well, let me say at the outset that I'm very conscious of our business partnership. We have worked together for many years. It has been profitable business for us and we trust that it has been profitable for you too.
	"We want to keep this relationship flowing and we look forward to carrying on business together to our mutual advantage.
	"We hope that we can find in this present cancellation an opportunity to reinforce our goodwill.
	"The interests of my company hinge on the fact that the order involved special design work and that we had booked production capacity to the exclusion of other potentially profitable business.
	"We have, of course, sought quickly to fill our production capacity but . . ."

Imagine David continuing to paint the picture as he saw it. Imagine how Charles might comment on the goodwill and might inform David of his company's view. Before they got into the controversial area of looking for a mutually acceptable cancellation fee, they had established that compared with their shared interest in maintaining their goodwill and their business relationship.

Analysis
Martin and Guy rushed their fences. They were very quickly into areas of controversy and antagonism. Before the word "goodwill" had been

mentioned, they were at loggerheads so that they obscured any search for a constructive outcome.

By the time Charles and David reached such possible controversy, it was in place as a trivial detail to be overcome within the context of their long-term association.

Charles and David understood the structure of a constructive negotiation.

SUMMARY

1. There are good reasons to create some structure for the conducting of a negotiation. It helps to:
   reduce ambiguity
   produce control
   empower the timing of statements
   progress only as matters ripen
   concentrate technique—different technique for different phases.
2. The structure we recommend for the subject matter is:
   Exploration
   Bidding
   Bargaining
   Settling
3. In constructive negotiations, it is particularly important to use the right technique for the opening phase: exploration.

EXERCISE

In this exercise, you should work with half a dozen fellow students. Three of you should represent the firm, and the remainder should be students in the exercise.

A team of three business studies students is going to negotiate the terms of a work-based project with a local engineering firm. The Polytechnic has not previously had a project with this firm. The students are to meet the Managing Director, his Personnel Manager in charge of training and the Accountant in whose department they expect to be working. All that has been done so far is that a tutor, in a telephone conversation with the Personnel Manager, has gained tentative agreement for a project to be carried out and has a suggestion that it should be in the general field of transfer pricing between departments.

The normal conditions for a Polytechnic project are:
   (a) A successfully completed project is an essential element in your course.
   (b) The four students will work on the project for six weeks full time.

(c) The firm is not expected to pay the students but to cover the cost of any materials used (including preparation of the final report) and to cover any agreed expenses necessarily incurred, e.g. travel between different sites, computer facilities, etc.

(d) The students must have access to any necessary information.

(e) At the end of the project the students will give a presentation to the management of the firm and provide a written detailed report. One bound copy of the report must be left in the Polytechnic library.

(f) Matters of confidentiality need to be agreed.

(g) There should be a contact inside the firm with an interest in the project and enough influence to open doors for the students where necessary.

(h) This is no guarantee of the standard of work to be done. This is primarily a learning exercise for the students.

With the limitations that the meeting should not last for more than 45 minutes, conduct a negotiation between the two sides.

Before Starting the Negotiation Read the Following:

Before entering the negotiations, both teams should answer the following questions, revealing their answers to each other after completing the negotiation.

1. What would be your key opening remark to establish mutual confidence?
2. Would you expect to complete all forms of the EBBS stages at this meeting?
3. If not, how far would you expect to get?
4. At a subsequent meeting with whom would you expect to negotiate?
5. Is there to be a further meeting?
6. What matters *must* be cleared up at the first meeting?

After Completing the Negotiation

Revert to your separate groups and in each discuss for ten minutes:

1. What was the climate of the negotiation? How was it formed? Could it have been better?
2. Was reasonable agreement reached from the outset on procedure?
3. In what stages was the subject-matter developed?

Finally

Join with the other group and compare your answers to the questions posed for you before you started and after you'd finished.

What do you learn

(a) From the exercise as a whole?

(b) From any differences of answers in the final part of the exercise?

FURTHER READING

There is a large literature dealing with stages in negotiation. Different writers identify the stages in different ways, and it is not entirely clear how the literature comes together. However, there is general agreement that:

1. Stages in negotiation may be divided into those which differentiate the positions of the parties and those which integrate the positions of the parties.

2. The techniques needed for differentiation are very different from the techniques needed for integration.

3. Negotiations cycle and recycle through stages involving differentiation and stages involving integration. To avoid unnecessary difficulties the progress through the stages needs to be carefully managed.

Useful introductions are given in:

Warr, P.B. (1973) *Psychology and Collective Bargaining.* London: Hutchinson.

Carlisle, J. & Leary, M. (1981) Negotiating groups. In Payne, R. & Cooper, C. (eds.), *Groups at Work.* Chichester: Wiley.

More advanced discussions are presented by:

Morley, I.E. & Stephenson, G.M. (1977) *The Social Psychology of Bargaining.* London: George Allen & Unwin.

Gulliver, P.H. (1979) *Disputes and Negotiations: A Cross-cultural Perspective.* New York: Academic Press.

For a treatment of stages in negotiation which treats the stages in negotiation as particular examples of more general stages in decision making see:

Morley, I.E. (1987) Negotiation and Bargaining. In Hargie, O. (ed.) *A Handbook of Communication Skills.* London: Croom Helm.

The stages are identified as identification (of issues), development (of solutions), and selection (of policies). I would now add implementation (of policies) as a stage requiring special attention.

For a treatment of stages in commercial negotiations which also attempts to recognize critical points in negotiation see:

Marsh, P.D.V. (1984) *Contract Negotiation Handbook.* London: Gower Press.

Scott, W.P. (1981) *The Skills of Negotiating.* Aldershot: Gower Press.

Argues that the phases of a negotiation provide one thread in the fabric of a negotiation. Other threads are lateral verses vertical approaches (dealing with issues on a broad front versus dealing with issues one at a time); the form of the confrontation (follow my leader versus independent sequencing); and the structure of concentration over the period of the negotiation.

CHAPTER 7
The Opening Phase: Exploration

INTRODUCTION

In considering constructive negotiation and after laying the foundations at the level of climate and the opening procedure, we are now moving into the subject matter. We start with the phase of exploration.

The plan for this chapter is:
1. The situation as we find it.
2. Some examples of development.
3. Analysis of those examples.
4. Suggested technique.

THE SITUATION

The parties have met and have established the chemistry of their personal relationships.

They have outlined and agreed on the procedure they will follow.

They have begun to bend towards one another but still have far to go.

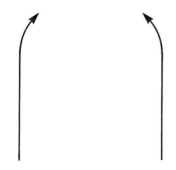

Fig. 7.1

They have created a basis from which they can move forward into a constructive and creative outcome.

But there is still danger of unnecessary controversy and conflict.

Let us take some examples.

47

EXAMPLES

An engineering concern in a developing country has been awarded a contract for a road-building programme. It is their first venture into road-building in that country. They have won a contract against the competition of another company, who are completing a contract for the predecessor road programme. Call them respectively New Company and Old Company.

New Company do not at present have the labour and equipment in this country which Old Company have.

What might happen if those two parties met?

Example 1

Old: "Well, come in. How can we help you?"

New: "Well, as you know, we have the contract to build the new phase of the road programme here and we would like to buy your equipment. We would like to know how much you would want for it."

Old: "Well, quite frankly, we are not thinking of selling it."

Example 2

After greetings:

New: "Well, thank you for agreeing to this meeting. I would like to talk to you about the road-building programme and the possibility that we could help you with the equipment that you have been using.

"We understand that you have a problem of having invested in a machine and not now having a use for it, and we would like to offer you the chance to sell it or loan it to us."

Old: "Ah, I see. You mean you need the equipment we have got? I'm afraid it's not for sale."

Example 3

After ice-breaking:

New: "Thank you for allowing me to come to this discussion. As I see it, we both have interests in the road programme in this country and I would like to explore with you whether there are opportunities which we could turn to our mutual advantage.

"Could we use a half hour informally to chat about this?"

Old: "Yes . . . yes, I think that might be interesting."

New: "If we find any points of common interest, we would presumably want to go away and think about it a bit and then get together again later on?"

Old: "Yes, by all means. What have you in mind?"

New: "Well, frankly, at this stage I have a very open mind. It seems to me that there should be possibilities. I have done a little thinking about them but they can't take any shape until you and I have this discussion.

"There seem to me to be both long-term and short-term opportunities.

"For example, at the moment we are thinking out our detailed plans for the contract which has recently been awarded to us. We appreciate that you have resources and experience which we don't have at present."

Old: "So . . . , you would like to discuss whether we could find some way to operate together over the next couple of years on this contract?"

New: "Yes, I'd like to discuss that, and I would also be interested to have some wider ranging discussion."

Old: "How do you mean?"

New: "Well, the next stage of the road programme will be coming up in a couple of years' time. Both of us are likely to put in tenders and to be looking over our shoulders worrying about what the other is going to do. I am not looking for any shady deals, but I am conscious that each of us could force the other into a non-profit situation.

"I would be interested to see if there is any open and constructive way in which we might, long term, both of us, make more profits than losses."

Old: "That is certainly interesting! Goodness knows it is tough enough to make any profit on these sort of jobs.

"Yes, I can see that it would be worth at least discussing the issue. Yes, by all means.

"How should we tackle it? Start with the issues that will be coming up in a couple of years' time, or start with today's issues?"

New: "Well, how would it be if we see whether we can find ways of working together on today's issues? That would give us a take-off point for longer term discussion."

Old: "Right, let's tackle it that way. Have you done any thinking about the possibilities for the short-term?"

New: "Yes, we have done a little thinking, but obviously not much before this discussion.

"Let me tell you how we are seeing things and then ask you for a first reaction.

"Our overall situation is that we have a world-wide development programme and in particular we have an objective of developing our market in this country. The road programme is a major step in that direction and we are, frankly, very pleased to have achieved the contract.

"Not that there is much profit in it. As you may guess, to win that contract against the competition of established and proven contractors in this country—yourselves—we have had to cut things to the bone.

"We are now aiming to make a thorough-going success of this phase and we are of course planning the ways in which we can mobilize the additional labour we would want and such equipment as we have not already got.

"We know that you have been using labour and equipment and we wonder whether you have yet decided how you will use it in the future or whether you would be open to some discussion about that . . ."

Old: "That's very interesting. Our position is, as you say, that we have labour and equipment that we have been using on the road programme. And of course we are at a stage of deciding how best to make use of that in future.

"How could we find ways to look after both sets of interests?"

Analysis

In the first example, the two parties were almost immediately at odds on the price of some equipment. The negotiation was heading rapidly for no-deal.

In the second, it was going to be at best a contentious and hard-fought battle.

In the final example, the parties were working together in their joint interests. It did not necessarily have to be by a sale of the equipment: they might have decided on anything in a panorama including sale, rental, sub-contracting and a host of other possibilities.

And they were looking forward to exploring the prospects for some longer term co-operation.

After ice-breaking and agreeing Purpose, a rough Plan, and Pace, they were reaching common goals by a careful and stimulating process of Exploration.

New Company's delegate stated his own position.

Having stated it, he then sat and listened to the Old delegate's viewpoint.

Each asserted his own interests. Neither contradicted the other nor sought to impose on the other. They negotiated constructively.

The situation is a familiar one. Whenever we meet other people, we have our own ideas and are often surprised to find out how their ideas can be so different. The differences are, of course, magnified in the possible confrontation of a negotiation.

Each of us starts with his own perception of the Other Party. His own knowledge, uncertainties, suspicions. Each has his own background: his own knowledge of his organization, of his organization's goals, attitudes and behaviours. His own objectives for the present negotiation. His own hopes and fears of how the negotiation may develop.

These are, at this stage, his own perception. They are not, at this stage, shared perceptions (Fig. 7.2).

Fig. 7.2

Soon we can see that the other party recognizes only a fraction of this picture (Fig. 7.3).

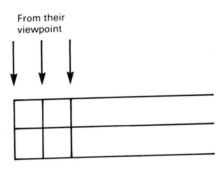

Fig. 7.3

But of course the other party also perceives many things which we don't (Fig. 7.4).

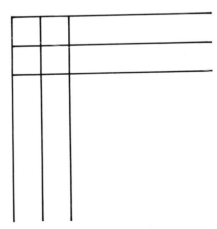

Fig. 7.4

51

There is, at the outset, some limited area in which both see things the same way. There is some further area in which one party has its own unique vision of things, and another area in which the Other Party has its distinctive vision.

And always there are aspects which neither perceives (Fig. 7.5).

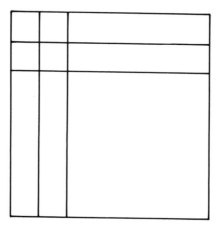

Fig. 7.5

In reality, it is hard for either to understand the other's perception.

Both parties have to work hard if they are to extend their vision. They have to work hard in conditions in which each is likely to be suspicious of the other. And each is likely to be so anxious to assert his own perception that he may not hear what the Other Party is saying. Not hear, let alone understand or accept.

But suppose that the Other Party is willing to give us some more information about what they're seeing (Fig. 7.6). Suppose that we

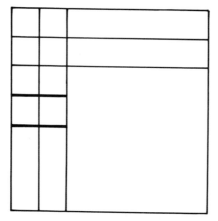

Fig. 7.6

manage to listen and to understand what they are saying.

Then, because our viewpoint is different from theirs, we can take a great leap forward (Fig. 7.7).

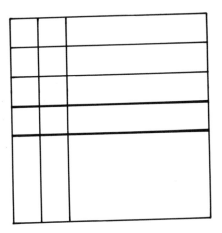

Fig. 7.7

If we can carry on the good work, both sharing information, then we can reach a point at which both of us see more in the same way (Fig. 7.8).

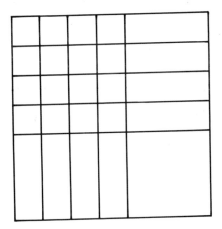

Fig. 7.8

Note particularly that there is an area which we can both see, which was previously obscured from us both (Fig. 7.9).

It is from this area—from the exploration that we can do together and

53

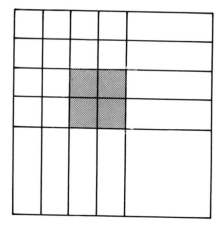

Fig. 7.9   A new area of common vision

from the new visions we can share—that the parties can together open up shared goals.

It takes hard work and skilful technique, but it can open up appetizing prospects for creative and constructive negotiation.

There are pitfalls.

If you tell me your view of things and it differs from mine, then I'll probably want to put you right. And then you will stand up for what you have said, and so we are in for an argument.

We will do much better if I listen to all you have to say and accept it, and summarize it to check that I have understood you properly.

And only then, quite independently, tell you my point of view.

You and I can understand that we have different points of view and we can cope with that, and we can still together look for creative possibilities.

What we cannot do is to tolerate challenges and contradictions from each other.

SUGGESTED TECHNIQUE

Please look again at the examples quoted earlier in this chapter.

The third dialogue opened up prospects for the negotiation which were obscured by the developments in the first two examples.

Here are some general guidelines for technique in this Exploration phase.

1. Be positive. Stress the positive aspects of your position. Stress your

interest in doing business with the others. Recognize obstacles as problems to be solved, not as barriers preventing progress.

2. Take the helicopter view. Rise above the details separating you today. Put them in the context of longer-term possibilities.
3. Listen. It's tempting to do most of the talking yourself. Try instead to cultivate the skill of effective listening.
4. Make independent statements. Avoid the pitfalls of challenge and contradiction.
5. Search with the Other Party for common goals. Focus on those things which you both agree to be in your joint interests.

This creative exploratory phase—founded on skilful laying of the foundations—is the critical element of *constructive* negotiating.

Successfully handled, this phase of Exploration is so important that subsequent phases pale into lower significance.

SUMMARY

1. Negotiators embark on the subject matter having (hopefully) laid appropriate foundations of climate and procedure.
2. They have kept to neutral ground. At the outset of the subject under discussion, they should still be increasing the impetus towards agreement—not yet at the toughest of problems.
3. Each has his own independent perspective.
4. The greater the extent to which they can form a shared perspective, the greater the prospect of recognizing fresh creative possibilities, and of reaching shared goals.
5. Key elements of technique for this phase are:

> Be Positive
> Make Independent Statements
> Listen
> Then seek together for Common Goals

EXERCISES

1. Refer back to the example at the end of Chapter 3 (re-painting the Students' Union Bar). As the Students' Union negotiator how do you perceive the problem? How would you expect one of the quoting firms to perceive the problem? Where do these perceptions agree?—clash?—not affect each other?
2. Think again about your experience in the exercise following Chapter

6. What differences of perspective were there between the teams? Both teams were working from the same briefing. What differences would you expect in reality?

FURTHER READING

Bellow, G. & Moulton, B. (1981) *The Lawyering Process: Negotiation.* New York: Foundation Press.
Contains a useful discussion of constructive negotiation under the heading "The Nature of Problem-Solving Bargaining" (pp. 150–157).

Video Arts (1985) *So You Think You Can Sell?* London: Methuen.
An important part of the attitudes of constructive negotiations is that they treat objections as opportunities. The Video Arts team show (in Chapter 1) that many objections can be anticipated in advance and countered with questions designed to make the objection as specific as possible.

Fisher, R. & Ury, W. (1983) *Getting to Yes: Negotiating Agreement Without Giving In.* London: Hutchinson.
Fisher and Ury give a very useful introductory treatment of problems of perception in negotiation groups (pp. 22–30). They also suggest a number of procedures which will help negotiators take what Bill Scott calls the helicopter view. Further discussion of problems of perception in negotiation is given in

Lockhart, C.L. (1979) *Bargaining in International Conflicts.* New York: Columbia University Press. Especially pp. 44–60.

Morley, I.E. (1981) Negotiating and bargaining. In Argyle, M. (ed.) *Social Skills and Work.* London: Methuen.

Morley, I.E. (1987) Negotiating and Bargaining. In Hargie, O. (ed.) *A Handbook of Communication Skills.* London: Croom Helm.

Winkler, J. (1981) *Bargaining for Results.* London: Heinemann/Institute of Marketing.
Contains very useful sections on setting up the deal, and probing and presenting.

Smith, V. (1987) Listening. In Hargie, O. (ed.) *A Handbook of Communication Skills.* London: Croom Helm.
Reviews what is known about the skills of listening.

Scott, W.P. (1981) *The Skills of Negotiating.* Aldershot: Gower.
Deals with the exploratory phase under headings of opening statements, the creative phase, strategy review, and issues. The exploratory phase should follow naturally from the climate already developed, reinforcing the gains which have already been made.

CHAPTER 8
Constructive Bidding and Bargaining

INTRODUCTION

In a constructive negotiation a great deal of early effort goes into establishing understanding and shared goals.

The process of constructive negotiation encourages the establishment and the development of positive attitudes from both parties. The phases of ice-breaking, procedural opening, and thorough exploration are carried out sensitively. Each party achieves a recognition of the other's interest and possibilities. The two parties come to share some common goals. The scene is set for rapid progress.

There is more to be done, but the established momentum is moving towards agreement.

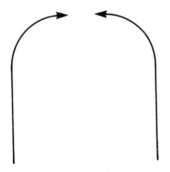

Fig. 8.1

The Bidding, Bargaining and Settling phases of a constructive negotiation are important, but not of the same dimension as their significance in competitive negotiation.

In a constructive negotiation, the dominant phase—both in time and significance—is Exploration.

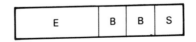

Fig. 8.2

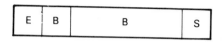

Fig. 8.3

In a competitive negotiation, the dominant phase is Bargaining.

Because of the relative weight of Bidding and especially of Bargaining in a competitive negotiation, we shall postpone detailed treatment of those phases until Part 2 of this book. Here in Part 1, we restrict our attention to a synopsis of those phases.

THE BIDDING PHASE

Based on the climate which has been established and based on the mutual search for common goals, Bidding for both parties becomes a well-informed stage. Each has formed an appreciation of the other's position and needs. Each is in a good position to anticipate a realistic settlement.

Suppose that David Stanton's factory had some waste paper to sell. If Tina Thorne called to see him, she would take time to find out the qualities David was offering, the quantities, the frequency, the storage conditions, anything else of importance to David. She would then make clear her own interests. She would then make a bid covering collection arrangements, quality guarantees, payment terms, based on the market price of £50.

If Martin McLean called on David, Martin would be eager to get quickly to the Bidding phase and to show his mettle. Knowing that the market price for waste paper was £50, he would offer £40 in the hope of reaching a deal at £45.

The guidelines for Bidding in a constructive negotiation are:

> Be realistic
> Within realism aim high
> State your bid firmly and authoritatively.

THE BARGAINING PHASE

When the earlier stages have led to understanding between the parties and when the bid has been realistic, many constructive negotiations need only a brief bargaining phase.

There are, inevitably, going to be occasions when there are differences between the parties; differences which have to be resolved through a process of Bargaining.

The attitudes of the parties during Bargaining are important. Within a constructive negotiation, there are attitudes of searching positively to reach agreed common goals, to the mutual advantage of both parties. Differences between them are obstacles to be overcome.

Contrast the position we will find when discussing competitive negotiation: each party dominantly concerned with his own interests, with wresting the best advantage for himself.

Guidelines for the Bargaining phase will be discussed in detail in Chapters 16 and 17. The key points to be mentioned in the context of constructive negotiation are:

Be positive
Avoid head-on collisions
Trade concessions. If you need to give a little, then get a little at the same time
Move at a measured pace. Don't expect instant solutions.

THE SETTLING PHASE

The phase of Settling is now approaching. It is important—as both parties sense its arrival—that they seize the moment, seize the available agreement, rather than trying to dot every 'i' and cross every 't'. Such detail can be sorted out in later correspondence. Delay over detail can prejudice the seizing of the available opportunity.

SUMMARY

1. In constructive negotiations, the foundations for agreement are carefully laid in the early stages.
2. Bidding and Bargaining do not begin until those foundations have been laid.
3. Bids in a constructive negotiation should be realistic and should be stated authoritatively.
4. The Bargaining phase in this style of negotiating becomes a constructive phase in which people with inevitably different requirements look together to see how they can resolve them.
5. The guidelines to these phases will be discussed in more detail in Chapters 16–19.

EXERCISE

1. What common ground would you look for in a negotiation in which you are seeking sponsorship for a town basketball team from a nationally known insurance company with its headquarters in your town?

FURTHER READING

McCall, J.B. & Warrington, M.B. (1984) *Marketing by Agreement: A Cross-Cultural Approach to Business Negotiations*. Chichester: Wiley.
Chapter 2 contains a useful analysis of the skills required at different stages of negotiation.

Fisher, R. & Ury, W. (1981) *Getting to Yes: Negotiating Agreement Without Giving In*. London: Hutchinson.
Discusses some of the principles which are likely to produce more creative agreements.

Walton, R.E. & McKersie, R.B. (1965) *A Behavioral Theory of Labor Negotiations*. New York: McGraw-Hill.
Much of Walton and McKersie's discussion of integrative bargaining (and some of the material on attitudinal structuring) may be used to expand Bill Scott's ideas.

CHAPTER 9

The Importance of Preparation

INTRODUCTION

In this first chapter on Preparation, we shall discuss why the subject is so important and suggest criteria for Preparation.

WHAT'S THE PROBLEM?

The context is a process of negotiating. A very complicated process. One in which negotiators can all too easily be submerged in a wealth of conflicting impressions and thoughts.

And yet, a process in which it is vital that they are alive to all that is going on, responsive and positive to rapidly moving circumstances. Recognizing both the general drift and the current detail and the implications. Constantly contributing to the development of the meeting, making constructive comments controlling the direction of the negotiation.

The human brain is a superb piece of equipment to tackle such complexity. Properly used, it can tackle intricate problems.

Poorly used, it becomes overloaded and unable to cope.

EXAMPLES

At breakfast time, I like to read the morning paper and my wife likes to talk about our day's programme.

If I go on reading I don't hear what she says, let alone understand or respond. I can't do both.

I can talk to my wife and she can engage in a conversation while she is knitting. All the mental energy can be given to the conversation.

She is an expert knitter and it does not need much mental energy to continue the mechanical process of simple knitting.

I can drive and I can map-read, but I can't do both efficiently at the same time.

If someone else is driving, I can map-read and give him instructions.

If I am driving on my own on a journey that I do not travel regularly, I need either a plan I have thought out previously or frequent stops to consult the map.

I find it easier to have prepared a simple, clear plan for the journey with a few intermediate points and road numbers printed boldly. A plan I can see at a glance.

If I am asked to make a proposal at a meeting on a topic which I know well, I sometimes make a mess of it.

I know the subject so well that I feel maybe I can get away without preparing it.

And I don't take the trouble to put my knowledge into shape.

And I make a mess of it.

COMMENTS

Those are all examples of ways of using our conscious energy, and of ways in which that energy can be overloaded.

Reading and listening both demand continuous energy. The human brain cannot concentrate on both concurrently.

One can concentrate on reading whilst performing another automatic function; just as one can for example listen while riding a bicycle. One can talk while driving a car unless one gets into a heavy traffic situation—one which demands conscious energy.

Negotiating is working in heavy traffic. One needs every element of help one can create to be able to drive efficiently through that traffic.

That's the problem. The negotiator's brain is likely to be overloaded.

SUGGESTED SOLUTIONS

There are two forms of help to cope with this overload. One form is to use mechanical processes as much as possible. For that reason, it is important for a negotiator to develop drills which he will use repeatedly.

For example, the drill of automatically following some ice-breaking formula at the start to establish a cordial climate. The drill of regularly using a particular form of opening procedure. The drill of full exploration before getting embroiled in later phases.

These drills become routine if—and only if—we can practise them repeatedly. We can only do this through experience and discipline. There is no substitute for the experience, even though some of it may be compressed in intensive seminars.

There is another vital element in being able to drive efficiently through the heavy traffic of a negotiation.

It is **being prepared**.

It should be axiomatic that any negotiator will do his technical homework in advance. The technical expert will research the specification, the quality requirements, the ability and reputation of potential suppliers. The seller's technical staff will make the corresponding technical examinations of their ability to supply. The buyer will absorb the reports on the technical negotiations and build his own panorama of budgets, delivery needs, terms, guarantees.

Each of us has his own specialist role and each of us needs to prepare his thinking in that specialist role.

The preparatory work for a negotiation needs to go further if it is to minimize the overload.

It must lead to a sharp and simple product. A guideline (or guidelines) sharp enough to stand as clear beacons.

There is an analogy with a person struggling to find his way home through the countryside on a dark night. If he (or she) has equipped himself in advance with a torch, he need not constantly be feeling for obstacles in the path.

If, in addition, he has established clear recognizable beacons along his path, he can make good progress.

If all is murky, no torch, no beacons, he's in for a rough night.

Preparation for negotiations should have an end-point which is sharp and simple as a series of beacons.

It needs to be sharp to the extent that it is wholly clear in one's subconsciousness.

It is no use, when confronted by the unexpected, having to extract a particular thought from a glutinous mass at the back of one's mind. That only adds to the overload.

Sharpness and simplicity are the hallmarks of effective preparation.

How are we to achieve such sharpness and simplicity? What is it that we should prepare so sharply, so simply? Those are the topics of Chapters 10 and 11.

SUMMARY

1. Negotiation is a complicated process.
2. It makes heavy demands on the conscious knowledge of every negotiator.
3. Unless he is skilled, the negotiator will be overburdened by this complexity.

4. He can reduce the load by using repetitive drills as much as possible.
5. He can free much of his conscious energy for the meeting if he arrives clear-minded and well prepared.

EXERCISE

1. Assess your own capacity to operate under overload. Spend a free hour on this task. Select jobs which you could normally be expected to tackle in the course of your week. For example:

   (a)   Reading a chapter of a textbook.
   (b)   Designing an evening meal for yourself and five flatmates.
   (c)   Writing a weekly letter home.
   (d)   Selecting a college sporting team of your own choice.
   (e)   Listing eight Desert Island Discs for the campus radio programme.
   (f)   Listing the clothes to take on a botanical field study weekend.
   (g)   Deciding with your boy/girlfriend where to go on holiday.
   (h)   Drafting the headings for a paper in your own subject to be presented to a tutorial group.

Try to get as much as you can of all these jobs done in the hour.
   At the end of the hour answer these questions:

   (a)   Roughly what percentage of each task did you complete?
   (b)   What feelings came to your mind during the hour? Jot down as many adjectives/phrases as you can.

FURTHER READING

Morley, I.E. (1987) Negotiating and Bargaining. In Hargie O. (ed.) *A Handbook of Communication Skills*. London: Croom Helm.
Explains some of the ways in which skilled negotiators take account of limitations in our ability to process information.

Morley, I.E. (1982) Preparation for Negotiation: Conflict, Commitment and Choice. In Bradstatter, H., Davis, J.H. & Stocker-Kreichgauer, G. (eds.) *Group Decision Making*. London: Academic Press.
Discusses the importance of preparation for negotiation. Particular attention is paid to problems of complexity in negotiation. It is shown that inadequate preparation makes constructive negotiation quite impossible. Much of the paper deals with advanced issues in the psychology of decision making.

Morrison, W.F. (1985) *The Pre-Negotiation Book*. Chichester: Wiley.
A how-to-do-it text which deals mainly with preparation for buying and selling.

Scott, W.P. (1981) *The Skills of Negotiating*. Aldershot: Gower.
The approach advocated is very similar to the approach set out in Scott's later book. The earlier treatment is still worth reading, however, because it provides additional examples, and because there is a very useful treatment of the special problems posed by negotiations which are extended and complex.

CHAPTER 10
Preparation: Method

INTRODUCTION

In this part of the book we are concerned with constructive negotiations and the present chapters concentrate on the homework one should do in advance of a constructive negotiation.

In this chapter we shall be concerned with how do we tackle it?—the method we should use for our preparations. We leave until the next chapter the issue of what aspects of the negotiation we should prepare for.

How do we tackle our preparations?

The need is to establish a sharp and simple pattern for what one will have to do. Otherwise, during the negotiation, one will be too overloaded.

In setting out to prepare one's thinking about a known subject, one is surprisingly likely to overload the brain even during the preparation processes.

EXAMPLES

Harold had completed a project. It was time to sit down and write his report on it.

He knew all about the subject. He had worked intensively on it for several months. He was soaked in it.

No problem.

So he sat down, wrote the word introduction and started to write the report.

A quarter of an hour later he seemed, surprisingly, to have dried up. He was not at all clear where he was going next and so he looked back to the beginning of the introduction to pick up the threads again.

The introduction he had just written looked dreadful. So awful that he had to start all over again.

And again and again.

Many students find the same problem when it comes to writing essays.

Ian faced a similar problem with an important speech to his Institution.

He was the expert called to make the presentation and was quite determined to make a first-class job of it.

He sat down to think it through a couple of months in advance and found himself quickly running into the same sorts of problems as Harold. He knew so much about the subject that he had difficulty in putting it into a reasonable sequence.

ANALYSIS

These experts, each capable in his own field, failed to make the best use of their talents. Each was unable to use his brain effectively. Each lacked the method for preparing his thinking. A way of using his brain to best advantage.

The human brain is an extremely good store for information.

The human brain is also an extremely good analytical tool.

And it is highly capable of transmitting whether it be thoughts onto paper or the spoken word.

But the brain is overloaded if we ask it at the same time to do two of these functions. It can fulfil its function of reaching into the storehouse. Or it can fulfil its analytical role.

It cannot competently do both at one and the same time.

To make effective use of the abilities, it is important to keep the tasks separate. Operate the storehouse at one time. Operate the analytical function at another.

And then, if we are going off to a negotiation, imprint a sharp and simple picture into the mind where it can be harboured and powerful through the hurly burly of a negotiation.

What does this mean in practice? One solution is to use a three-stage process to get one's thinking in order. Let us call it the A4/A5/A6 method.

Stage 1
Stage One is a mind-clearing exercise, reaching into the storehouse and getting the ideas out of there and into writing.

Take an A4 sheet of paper. Sit down and think about your subject and attempt to capture on paper every idea that comes into mind.

The mind is so fertile that you do not have time to write down every idea as it comes. You have to use one, possibly two, words for each idea. This is the classic brain-storming approach. In a very concentrated period, not more than two minutes, concentrate on capturing the whole range of your thinking on your subject. Writing furiously and without concern for logic or order. Capture the whole range.

You will find that within a couple of minutes you have two full columns of words (Fig. 10.1).

The A4 sheet has now served its main purpose. It has helped you to clear your mind for the next stage.

The A4 is, in some sense, a stock of information on which you could call, but I find that this is a trap. If I refer to the A4, then I am tempted to use it all and my consciousness is full of this range of information. My energy is not then free to concentrate on the planning I need to do. I find it more useful simply to set the A4 aside or even to throw it into the waste paper basket so that my consciousness is released to concentrate on the next stage, the analytical stage.

In discussing that stage for the moment we are going to concentrate on the information that you will need to present. There are other aspects of what you should prepare in advance of a negotiation, but we won't worry about them until the next chapter. Concentrate for the moment on the information you need to present.

Stage 2

Take a sheet of A5 paper (A4 folded in half). Now relax, lean back in your chair and think.

Think of your prospective Other Party.

Do **not** think of what you are going to say. Think of what the other party will need to hear.

Note this basic attitude. Your preparation should not be of what **you** know, but of what **he** will need to want to receive.

Think of him. What do you know of his company? His job? His knowledge of your company and your products? Do you know what sort of chap he is personally? What does he know about this matter you are going to talk to him about? What will he want to know? What will he need to know?

What are the four headlines of importance for him?

Take your time about it. No rush at all now. These are the critical moments.

Your mind will now find it relatively easy to generate four or five headlines.

Four is the number to aim for. Not six, or seven, or eight. If you are coming up with more than four, think again, do a bit of coalescing, get down to four.

Once you have the simplicity of four such headlines, you will find it easy to put them into a sensible sequence.

Having established the four headlines, think of the sub-headings that you will use under each headline. Two or three supportive sub-headings for each (Fig. 10.2).

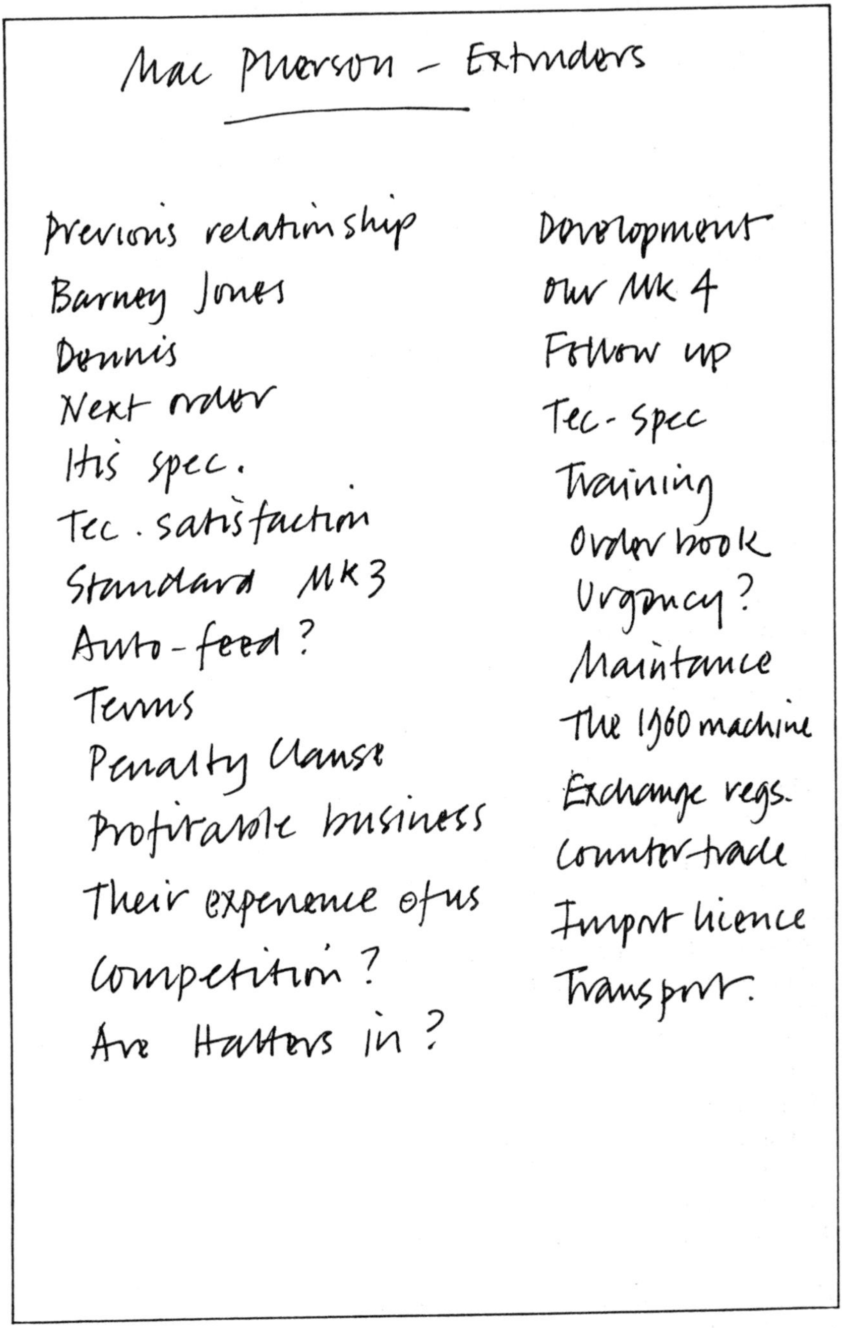

Mac Pherson — Extruders

Previous relationship	Development
Barney Jones	Our Mk 4
Dennis	Follow up
Next order	Tec - spec
His spec.	Training
Tec . satisfaction	Order book
Standard MK 3	Urgency ?
Auto-feed ?	Maintance
Terms	The 1960 machine
Penalty Clause	Exchange regs.
Profitable business	Counter-trade
Their experience of us	Import licence
Competition ?	Transport.
Are Hatters in ?	

Fig. 10.1   The A4: the brainstorming stage

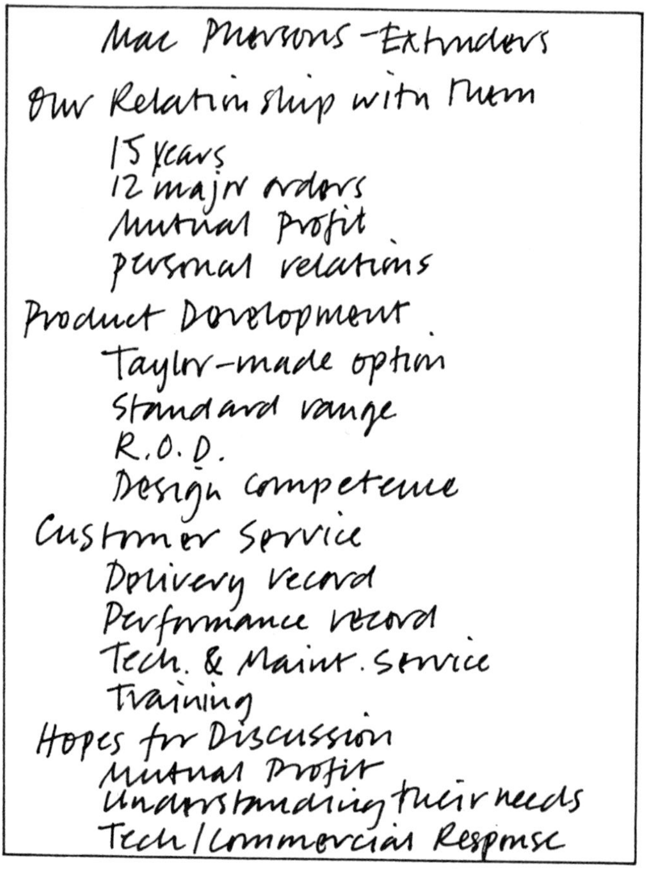

Mac Phersons – Extruders
Our Relationship with them
15 years
12 major orders
Mutual profit
personal relations
Product Development
Taylor-made option
Standard range
R.O.D.
Design competence
Customer Service
Delivery record
Performance record
Tech. & Maint. service
Training
Hopes for Discussion
Mutual Profit
Understanding their needs
Tech/Commercial Response

Fig. 10.2   The A5: four headlines plus support

Why this insistence on four? Because four is the number which the human mind can get into sharp focus. Four is the number which the mind can keep sharp later, as one wants to present the information in the hurly-burly of the negotiation.

Three or five may be tolerable, but my experience of sometimes trying to use more is that four is the maximum that my mind can comfortably keep sharp.

A psychologist friend once hinted that the concept of four could be theoretically justified. At a later stage, he recanted and claimed it was seven. But seven does not work for me!

In Stage 2 of the preparation of our message, we have developed an A5 which has on it four headlines, each backed by supporting sub-headings.

Stage 3
The final stage of the preparation process is to reduce the A5 picture to that minimum which will leave a sharp and simple imprint within the mind.

Readily accessible during the hurly-burly that you will soon be in.

Take another sheet of A4, fold it in four so that you have an A6.

Choose one key word for each of your four headlines. Print it large and clear on your A6 sheet.

So large and clear that if you want to pull it out of your pocket during the negotiation, it will take just one glance of the eyes to see the whole picture (Fig. 10.3).

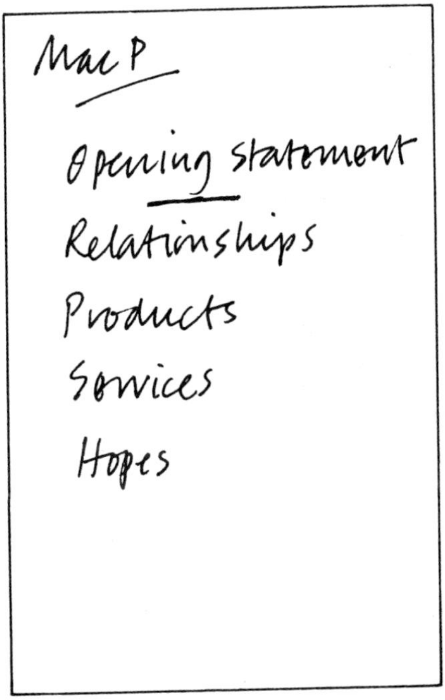

Mac P

Opening statement

Relationships

Products

Services

Hopes

Fig. 10.3   The A6: stark and simple

The end product of this preparation process is, in one sense, four words printed large on an A6—on a postcard if you like.

The more important product is a mind cleared in readiness for the situation one will soon be entering, with a sharp and simple imprint of the message one wants to send.

SUMMARY

1. The mind is all too easily overloaded even during preparation. It needs a systematic routine to make the most of one's thinking capacity.
2. We recommend a three-stage approach: A4/A5/A6.
3. Stage 1 is the A4—a concentrated brain-storming stage. One word per idea at random.
4. Stage 2 is the A5, the analytical stage, listener-oriented. Four headlines with supporting sub-headings.
5. Stage 3 is the simplification, the A6. Four key words printed large.

EXERCISE

1. Refer back to the negotiation on a student project after chapter 6. Using the A4/A5/A6 method, prepare the information you will want to give in the forthcoming negotiation, assuming that you are one of the student team.

FURTHER READING

Fisher, R. (1971) *Basic Negotiating Strategy: International Conflict for Beginners*. London: Penguin.
It is no accident that this book begins with a chapter headed "Think first about their decision". As Bill Scott says, much of your preparation should concern what the other side needs to know. It is also worth asking what operational decisions you might ask from them, and what they might ask from you. It is all too easy to become confused about what might be accomplished, and how. Chapter 2 of Fisher's book is entitled "Give Them a Yesable Proposition". It is also important to ask what yesable proposition they might ask from you.

Video Arts (1985). *So You Think You Can Sell*. London: Methuen.
Shows that one purpose of preparation is to identify questions designed to find out whether what the other side says is the issue really is the issue.

Winkler, J. (1981) *Bargaining for Results*. London: Heinemann.
See the chapter "Laying the Foundations for Results".

Rackman, N. & Carlisle, J. (1978) The Effective Negotiation—Part 2. Planning for Negotiations. *Journal of European Industrial Training* **2** (7) 2–5.
That skilled negotiators pay considerable attention to common ground when setting up their headings.

Scott, W.P. (1981) *The Skills of Negotiating*. Aldershot: Gower.
Divides planning into three stages concerned with ideas, with a thesis sentence, and with further analysis of the negotiating plan.

CHAPTER 11
Preparation: Content

INTRODUCTION

In the context of constructive negotiations we have seen the essential need to be well prepared and we have suggested a method to get our thinking into order.

This chapter concentrates on: What aspects of the negotiation should be prepared for?

We are specifically concerned with constructive negotiating processes. Different considerations will arise when we come to prepare our minds for a competitive negotiation. That will be discussed in Chapter 20.

THE NEED

What is it that you need to think through in advance of a negotiation? The information you have to give? More than that?

The mind must be so well prepared that it can be alert to new information, able to interpret and move forward with that fresh understanding, and able to control the direction that the negotiation takes.

In a constructive negotiation the vital part of the negotiation is the exploratory phase. Let us concentrate on preparing for that.

There are at least three dimensions in which it is sensible to prepare one's thinking.

Consider the different functions which your brain is called upon to perform during that vital stage.

1. There is a need to feed in a picture of your own perception of the negotiating ground.
2. There is a need to receive the Other Party's perception of that same ground—or rather, that similar ground.
3. There is a need then to join together creatively, to look for optimum possibilities in the situation.

This all too often takes place in a confused sequence and the mind is restlessly concerned—inarticulately concerned—about the obscurity of the process which is going on. This ambiguity is an additional stress.

If you prepare your brain simply to give information, then inevitably you will concentrate throughout the negotiation on projecting that information. Your brain will be blocked from receiving other different information.

For example, I was at a negotiation with a veteran negotiator, an extremely skilful one, the Purchasing Director of a major oil company. He was negotiating the purchase of £1½ million of chains for an oil rig (a relatively minor matter for him to be involved in). There were questions of size and price and specification and delivery, and a dozen other concerns. He was heavily involved in thinking of all those concerns and of discussing them and bargaining with a supplier.

It was a messy negotiation and, as we looked back on it subsequently, it turned out that he was not aware of the supplier's intention to supply in two different grades. He was so engrossed in thinking about other matters that he had never heard that intention mentioned. Yet I had heard it mentioned three times. It was certainly not because he is stupid—he is a brilliant man. It was simply that his brain was overloaded and it was not receiving.

It was an example which one rarely has the opportunity to witness in real life, but I find the same pattern repeated regularly in working seminars. Negotiators often do not hear.

If the first element of your preparation is the information you will present, then the second should be your planning to be a good listener.

A third aspect is to prepare for the conduct of the negotiating process. You should think through in advance the purpose of the proposed negotiation, your plan for tackling it and the time which you think it should take.

You can prepare yourself for three aspects:

To be a competent transmitter.
To be a competent receiver.
To have your plan for the process of the meeting.

We cannot prepare for the productive, creative phase which follows the early exploration. That is something that has to be spontaneous between the parties then and there. But by preparing properly, as far as we can, we can go into the negotiation in such a way that we will lead through with our minds alert and looking forward to this creative phase.

Before suggesting practical steps to cover these three aspects, there are two caveats.

First, this book concentrates on the skills of negotiating. It assumes technical competence in your own profession, be it accountant, technologist, banker, engineer or whatever. It assumes that you will have done your homework in that specialism.

Second, this part of the book concentrates on constructive negotiations. The key to a constructive negotiation is the phase of exploration and this chapter concentrates on the preparation for that phase. Other forms of preparation are needed for later phases.

PRACTICE

I regularly use a special practice for preparation for constructive negotiations. It is a three-stage process. The product is three A6s:

The first for the opening statement that one will present.
The second to prepare the mind for effective listening during the negotiation.
The third to prepare a plan.

The end points are:
The A6 for the opening statement. The information which I expect the Other Party to want or need prepared as discussed in the previous chapter. (See Figure 10.3.)
The listener's A6. Four key words, one key word for each of the four headline questions I would like to find answered by Other Party early in the negotiation. I follow the same general sequence of brain-storming (A4), analyzing (A5), and reducing to simplicity (A6), but this time applying my mind to its task as a listener. (See Figure 11.1.)
The procedural A6. This has on it three Ps: Purpose, Plan and Pace. What is the purpose of this negotiation I am going to? Is it to reach some agreement today or is it purely exploratory, or is it to resolve some difficulty, or is it a routine progress review? What is the Purpose?

What is my Plan—what sort of agenda would be sensible? Can I organize my thinking on that Plan under four main headings?

Pace—how long should it take?

A convenient end-point for this preparation is to take an A4 sheet and fold it into four. This creates, as it were, a four page booklet of A6 size. On page one I put the word PROC (for Procedure) and underneath three Ps.

Opposite the first P, I put that one word which is the key to the Purpose of the meeting. Opposite the second P, I put those four key words which headline the Plan for the meeting. And opposite the third P, I put the Pacing—the time one anticipates for the meeting.

On the back page, page four, I put the word Questions followed by one key word for each of the four headline questions (Fig. 11.2).

Inside, on page three, I put the letters O S (standing for Opening Statement) and four key words to remind me of the headline for that presentation.

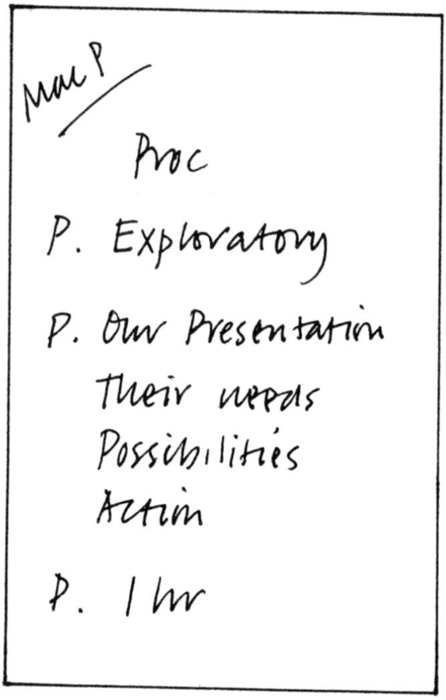

Fig. 11.1   A procedural A6

Page two is usually blank and is a suitable place on which I can write key figures—the very few really key figures which I am sure to want during the negotiation.

This tiny four-page reminder is in an inside pocket when I go to a negotiation. Usually, it stays there. The process of preparing it has made me prepare my mind and these headlines are usually stored firmly in my brain. Usually, I do not need the bit of paper to remind me but it is comforting to have it in my pocket and to be able to pull it out should I feel myself stumbling.

If you want to test this approach, how should you go about it?

Try repeatedly following the A4/A5/A6 method. First for Procedure, then for Questions, then for your Opening Statement. It may take an hour and a half the first time you try it.

The second time, you will be beginning to get the hang of it; you can manage it in an hour. The third time it will be still less. And once the practice is familiar, you will find yourself able to use it within half an hour.

One product is the little A6 booklet, something you can tuck into your

Fig. 11.2   A "questions" A6

pocket. The more important product is not the piece of paper. It is the simplicity and the clarity in your mind. The ability to use your energy purposefully during the negotiation. With minimum overload.

SUMMARY

1. The mind needs to be prepared in advance of a negotiation.
2. Prepared to transmit information.
3. Prepared to receive information.
4. Prepared to plan and control the development of the meeting.
5. The four-page booklet symbolizes the mind ready prepared for each of those tasks.

EXERCISE

1. Complete your preparation for negotiation begun after Chapter 9 by preparing
   (a)   your opening statement
   (b)   your listening preparation
   (c)   your procedural preparation—Purpose, Plan and Pace.

FURTHER READING

Morley, I.E. (1987) Negotiating and Bargaining. In Hargie, O. (ed.) *A Handbook of Communication Skills*. London: Croom Helm.
Provides further illustration of the idea that negotiators have limited mental capacities. If one task takes a lot of mental effort they may not be able to do another at the same time. This is one reason why negotiation is sometimes described as the dialogue of the deaf.

Morrison, W.F. (1985) *The Prenegotiation Planning Book*. Chichester: Wiley.
Argues that comprehensive preparation is a must. His own scheme has participants complete a 25-item checklist linked to a planning spread sheet. Bill Scott's procedures do the same kinds of job, and are easier to use.

Rackham, N. & Carlisle, J. (1978) The Effective Negotiator—Part 2. Planning for Negotiations. *Journal of European Industrial Training* **2** (7) 2–5.
Shows that skilled negotiators are more likely than average negotiators to plan in terms of a range of possibilities. Less skilled negotiators tend to get trapped into thinking about a fixed point.

Hawkins, K. (1979) *A Handbook of Industrial Relations Practice*. London: Kogan Page.
Provides a very useful, concise account of the kind of planning needed in industrial relations bargaining.

CHAPTER 12

Timing and Control

INTRODUCTION

There are two more chapters to complete this part of the book on Constructive Negotiation. In the first, to complete the framework, we shall be concerned with procedure after the introductory stage of the negotiation. Then in a final chapter with some negotiating tactics.

This chapter starts with sections on Timing and on Control, followed by examples and comments.

TIMING

A sense of timing is a key element in negotiating.

There is first the time profile of a negotiation which we have previously seen. In particular, there is the high significance of the opening and closing phases (Fig. 12.1).

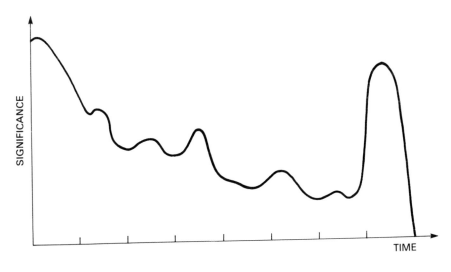

Fig. 12.1

Second, we have already emphasized the importance of discriminating between the successive phases:

Exploration

Bidding

Bargaining

Settling

It is important to time the movement from one phase to the next. In constructive negotiations, be particularly careful to complete Exploration before Bidding.

Third, there is the concept of ripeness. The time is not ripe to move from one of the above phases to the next until the former phase is really complete.

It is equally important to grasp issues while they are ripe. For example, when the Other Party is pressing you for higher quality, the time is ripe to establish the value of that higher quality.

Fourth, it is important to use time efficiently. It is all too easy to squander time on trivialities whilst ignoring things of higher importance.

To make effective use of time, the negotiators have to be in control of the way they are using time.

CONTROL

Negotiators become so involved with the subject matter of their negotiations, that often they have insufficient energy to keep control. The development of the negotiation is encumbered by this lack of control—by not pausing to check what progress is being made or how much time is being used.

There is a need periodically to summarize progress to date, to check that both parties agree on what they have so far done, to check on their use of time.

Such checks are easiest if there is a starting point of an agreed plan. You can agree how efficiently you are working if you can compare what you are achieving with some shared idea of what you should be achieving. It is more difficult if you lack that yardstick for comparison.

EXAMPLES

Sara Brady had an opportunity to negotiate a sale in Turkistan. There seemed to be possibilities of a big deal and she went out for three weeks.

When she arrived the decision to spend three weeks seemed very well justified. There was tremendous movement over the first two or three days. All very exciting.

The pace slackened off during the second week and it was becoming frustrating.

Week three saw matters getting worse and worse. Sara and the Turkistanis were both exasperated. So many small details were proving difficult. Sara despaired. It seemed to have been a waste of three weeks' desperately hard work. And so it went on until about 5 o'clock on Thursday afternoon, the day before she was due to leave.

Suddenly things began to bubble.

Now there was progress. Everybody got involved. Refreshments were sent for and the negotiations ran on into the evening . . . into the night . . . until 2 o'clock in the morning.

They started again at 7 o'clock and then continued in the taxi to catch the 2 o'clock flight from the airport.

Sara was frustrated, and so were the Turkistanis, by the inevitable low energy of weeks two and three. They were delighted with the sudden progress at the end.

David Stanton went to see the Turkistanis a couple of months later. He too booked a three-week trip, but planned to spend two weeks of that time with other clients in the Far East. He spent the first four days in Turkistan and had a highly successful time. There were several details still to be settled but he had allowed a 24-hour stop-over during his return trip.

After two weeks' profitable business further East—not to mention some fishing and some golf with his contacts—he stopped in Turkistan on the way back. After another highly productive day, David was on his way home with the contract signed.

There were of course details still needing to be hammered out, but David arranged for a member of his staff to fly out for two days to discuss those.

David knew all about the energy lapse in later stages of a negotiation. He planned not to waste time during that period.

The Operations Director of a services company is in the business of leasing out marquees. Much of their business is on long-running contracts where the details are re-negotiated annually.

It is the sort of situation in which the headline for most negotiations might read 'Same procedure as last year plus 5 per cent for inflation'. It might be expected that such a negotiation would take less than an hour. In practice, the realistic negotiator sets aside two hours and finds that there is always pressure so that a third hour is needed.

"The thing which astonishes me is that the great majority of the time is taken up on trivial details. If I am negotiating a £100,000 contract, we seem to take hours on triviality. Last week it was the cost per hour of repairing damaged canvas. It usually comes to something like £2,000 or £3,000 in a £100,000 contract.

"Last week we spent nearly the whole time arguing about the rate for canvas repairs. We ended up with an increase of only 3 per cent instead of the inflationary 5 per cent but I was not too worried—the 9 per cent increase we were seeking on the £100,000 contract otherwise went through without a murmur.

"I never cease to be amazed at the way most negotiations focus on the insignificant."

David Stanton has a range of questions that he keeps popping into discussions every 15 or 20 minutes:

"Where have we got to?"
"What have we agreed so far?"
"How is the time going?"
"What sort of progress are we making?"
"What should we be turning our attention to now?"
"I feel very involved about this item, but I wonder if it is really all that important?"

David has made a routine of using such questions to check progress regularly.

COMMENTS

Timing and Control are very important issues.

Any negotiator becomes so involved in negotiating the subject matter that there is a tendency for control to be lost.

I find that many negotiators who believe that the Other Party deliberately wastes time so as to sap their energy. It is a comment I heard made several times by negotiators who go to negotiations in China. They think it is a Chinese trick to slow down progress until they are almost due to catch their 'plane home.

Talking to Chinese, I find that they think that slow progress is a tactic used by Westerners to sap Chinese energy.

My belief is that this is not a cultural problem between Chinese and Western negotiators: it is simply the low phase in the energy profile of any negotiation.

It is difficult to keep control when one's mind is deeply involved in subject-matter. There are some elements of technique which can help.

1. Being well-prepared. Having a plan for the meeting.
   Having a schedule for its development. Having that plan and schedule reduced to a sharp and simple picture.

2. Having drills and routines which one can follow regularly.

What else can one do to keep control?

If negotiating in teams, it pays for one member to have responsibility for the procedural development of a meeting and for looking after the planning and control foundation on behalf of his colleagues.

When negotiating on your own, it is very tough. One solution is to develop the art of using a Control Question every 20 minutes or so. (See the examples ascribed to David Stanton above.)

It is even worth developing the discipline: as your watch shows the hour, and twenty past and twenty to, think of the word 'Control'.

SUMMARY

1. Negotiations readily drift unless they are kept under control.
2. The drift is inefficient.
3. The drift is energy sapping. The ambiguity of not knowing where we are or where we are going, adds to the negotiator's overload.
4. One effect is excessive attention to the insignificant.
5. There is a time profile of the development rate of a negotiation.
6. The knack of keeping control is not easily acquired. It has to be zealously developed.

EXERCISE

1. Put yourself back in the seventeenth century. You have been challenged to a duel and are negotiating the arrangements. Following on from what you have read in Chapter 12, what points of detail are likely to absorb you and distract you from the process of negotiation?

FURTHER READING

Gulliver, P.H. (1979) *Disputes and Negotiations: A Cross-Cultural Perspective.* New York: Academic Press.
Provides a very comprehensive (advanced level) discussion of stages in negotiation. He argues that progression through stages has a certain natural logic. Professional negotiators know this. Further, Gulliver reports that "They quite often alluded to a particular phase, to kinds of behaviour appropriate or inappropriate in it, to its purpose, and to the results expected from it" (p. 175). Perhaps the most important point to note is that "Attempts to short-cut the process pattern, through ignorance, inexperience, and the desire for haste, can lead to serious difficulties, more prolonged negotiations, damage to interests, and perhaps breakdown" (p. 175).

Carlisle, J. & Leary, M. (1981) Negotiating Group. In Payne, R. & Cooper, C. (eds) *Groups at Work*. Chichester: Wiley.
Reaches similar conclusions to Gulliver. Gives some practical advice about timing and control based on the findings of the Huthwaite Research Group.

Walton, R.E. (1969) *Interpersonal Peacemaking: Confrontations and Third Party Consultation*. Reading, Mass.: Addison-Wesley.
Discusses the process skills needed to manage deteriorating relationships. Many of the issues discussed are issues of timing and control.

CHAPTER 13

Constructive Tactics

INTRODUCTION

This is the final chapter in the part on Constructive Negotiations.

Negotiation tactics are a popular subject and are the subject of books galore. The majority of the tactics in those books are clever devices aimed at getting leverage over an opponent. Those sort of tactics may be appropriate for Competitive Negotiations and they will be dealt with in Part 2 of this book.

This chapter is confined to two tactics which are appropriate in Constructive Negotiations.

EXAMPLES

Martin and Guy, our young negotiating friends, found themselves exasperated.

They had met at 4 o'clock to discuss compensation for a cancelled contract, each thinking that the matter was reasonably simple and should be settled in half an hour. It wasn't.

It wasn't settled by 4.30 or even 5.30.

"Well," said Guy. "I must go now. I've got to pick up a new fishing rod before the shops close."

"Really," replied Martin. "I'm quite keen on fishing myself. I was just off to Martin Brook."

An hour later, they were fishing together. As darkness descended they went to The Horse & Farrier and shared a pie and a pint. Before they broke up for the evening, they had inevitably surveyed their earlier negotiations and agreed to continue them first thing in the morning.

The fishing, and the pie and the pint played their roles in enabling their respective companies to reach a settlement.

At least as important was the fact that Martin and Guy had quit the negotiating table at the right moment.

Tina and Sara had several years' experience in negotiating. When they met to discuss a contract for the disposal of waste paper, they found they could quickly agree on specification, on quality control, on penalty clauses and on deliveries. But they found themselves a long distance apart when it came to price and to terms of settlement.

Rather than thrash out those issues there and then, they took a 20-minute break.

When they met again, they found themselves summarizing their agreement and discussing not only price and settlement terms, but also examining discount possibilities.

There was new vitality in the negotiations.

Tina and Sara both knew the value of taking a break, a recess, during their negotiation.

Charles and David, highly experienced, make a point of taking regular breaks during their negotiations. At least an hour.

Sometimes they go off for a walk together and talk about the architecture around the block.

At other times when they break, and go to separate offices where each can re-think and re-plan and re-build his energy.

COMMENTS

A recess enables each party to review progress.

It enables each party to review their plans for the development of the negotiation.

It allows energy to be re-kindled.

It is taken at a point when energy is ebbing and provides for a new start at a higher level.

A couple of points about technique. The suggestion of a recess leads to a brief—very brief—spurt of fresh energy as people feel they have come to the end of this phase of negotiation.

Within seconds the energy level is going to sink from the new peak, even lower than before the suggestion was made.

Do not delay. Do not try to get just one more item articulated before we break. Break **now**.

On resumption after the recess, there is again a short spell of high energy involvement. Use it carefully.

Restore the climate with a mini ice-breaking. Restore the procedure; new agreement on Purpose, Plan and Pace.

Summarize agreement from the earlier phase.

Re-start with fresh exploration and search for further common goals. Make positive use of the refreshened climate.

When the climate in the negotiating room loses the cordial and co-operative mood that we want, take the negotiation out of the negotiating room. Take it into some environment where cordiality and co-operation are paramount.

Americans find it in the golf club. Englishmen find it over a good dinner, or in a pub, or in a Gentlemen's Club. If you are in Finland, it's in the sauna. If you are in Japan, it's in the bath-house. Wherever it is in your district, take the negotiation there.

SUMMARY

1. Constructive negotiators avoid destructive tactics.
2. One tactic always positive is the Recess.
3. Golden rules for the recess are: break quickly; re-start with a mini opening (ice-breaking, procedural opening, summary, fresh exploration).
4. If the mood of a negotiation becomes fraught, take it to a more positive environment; use the golf club tactic.

EXERCISE

When would you use the recess and when the golf club tactic during a negotiation?

PRACTICAL EXERCISE

The following should be undertaken by two teams each with two members. If you have other people available, there should also be two observers. The rules are as follows.

TEAM 1: You are the Finance Committee of the Students' Union. A benefactor has given directly to the Students' Union the sum of £100,000 towards the establishment of an outdoor pursuits centre to be run by the Students' Union. He has also left you 25 acres of land in a National Park suitable for climbing, canoeing and adventure training. This is located 40 miles from your college. You estimate that you can use all of the money on equipment and building at the site but recognize the need to make some prior arrangements. You will need a small office at the college, transport, and the permission of the authority to register the new club for which you estimate you will need a nominal membership fee and a visitor's charge for each day at the centre. In your estimate, the running costs of the site will be £25,000 per annum and the net cost of meals and accommodation for one person for one day will be £8.

The college has an unused office (16′ × 20′) equipped with desk and filing cabinet which will be admirable for your purpose and also has a 12-

seater minibus which had been bought for a now defunct club and is surplus to requirements.

TEAM 2: You represent the college authorities and are discussing setting up an outdoor pursuits centre by the Students' Union which has been given £100,000 for this purpose. You understand that they want to negotiate for the use of an office and the purchase of a minibus, both of which are available. The most recently let office accommodation was let at a rent of £5 per square foot per annum; the office you have in mind is 15' × 20' and is furnished. The minibus is depreciated down to £500 in the books although you have been offered £2,200 by a motor trader for it.

You are mainly concerned regarding the way in which the centre is to be run. You must satisfy yourselves that:

(a)   The college has no legal responsibility but that there is a strict control of safety because any malpractice would reflect on you.
(b)   The documents to govern the running and finance of the centre are sufficiently explicit. Past experience suggests a legal bill of the order of £2,000 to get this right.
(c)   There will be no financial call on the college in either setting up or running the centre.

ACTION

The teams should take about 30 minutes preparing for the negotiation and then 40 minutes negotiating. One observer should be attached to each team and sit with them during the preparation period. Each observer should sit in the background during the negotiation and, after the negotiation has ended, should feed back opinions on:

(a)   Whether their team has achieved its objectives.
(b)   How each team handled the different stages of the negotiation following an EBBS model, and communicating on climate and planning/control.
(c)   What bids were made and bargains struck.
(d)   Which were the major obstacles to agreement: how were they tackled and how were they overcome.

With or without the help of observers, the teams should discuss what they learn from the exercise. Discuss this, both within each team and between the teams.

FURTHER READING

Carlisle, J. & Leary, M. (1981) Negotiating Groups. In Payne, R. & Cooper, C. (eds) *Groups at Work*. Chichester: Wiley.

Confirm the importance of two of the tactics discussed by Bill Scott: summarizing and taking a break. Much of the chapter builds on work reported earlier in:

Rackham, N. & Carlisle, J. (1978) The Effective Negotiator—Part 2. Successful Negotiations. *Journal of European Industrial Training* **2** (6), 6–10.

Rackham, N. & Morgan, T. (1977) *Behavioural Analysis in Training.* Maidenhead: McGraw-Hill.
Report analyses the behaviour of experienced chairmen rated as effective by group members and by expert judges. One main finding was that the chairmen engaged in very high levels of activity designed to frame a decision: e.g. testing understanding and summarizing.

Whittington, D. (1986) Chairmanship. In Hargie, O. (ed.) *A Handbook of Communication Skills.* London: Croom Helm.
Underscores the importance of planning to have breaks for coffee, for walks, or whatever is needed to keep people alert.

Morley, I.E. & Stephenson, G.M. (1977) *The Social Psychology of Bargaining.* London: George Allen & Unwin.
Chapter 7 suggests the importance of treating the location of the negotiation as part of the system of communication.

Scott, W.P. (1981). *The Skills of Negotiating.* Aldershot: Gower Press.
Outlines eight tactics designed to foster collaboration towards a joint agreement.

SUMMARY OF PART 1

Part 1 of this book has been concerned with Constructive Negotiations: negotiations in which the attitudes of the parties are to search for agreement in their joint interests. Towards the development and constant care of business partnerships.

The first foundation level for these negotiations is to establish a climate which is cordial, co-operative, brisk and businesslike.

The second level of foundation is to have some procedure agreed between the parties. At the outset, agree on Purpose, Plan and Pace. As the negotiation develops, agree on progress and control the use of time.

In the subject matter, the key phase is that of Exploration. The later phases of Bidding, Bargaining and Settling are important, but not so crucial as in other styles of negotiating.

Preparation is vital. Preparation of one's knowledge, preparation of one's thinking. Developing one's thinking into sharp, simple patterns so that one reduces overloading at the negotiating table. Preparation of what one will say, plus preparation of what one will want to listen to, and preparation of one's procedure.

Use tactics which are to mutual advantage: the Recess and the Golf Club.

PART 2

COMPETITIVE NEGOTIATION

INTRODUCTION TO PART 2: COMPETITIVE NEGOTIATION

The time is ripe for us to consider a different style of negotiating.

This different style, called the Competitive style, is characterized by different values and attitudes in the negotiators. These in turn lead to differences of behaviour and of technique in the early stages of the negotiation.

Those aspects of a Competitive negotiation—values, attitudes and behaviour in the early stages—are the subject of Chapter 14.

Subsequently, we will need to delve deeper into the Bidding, Bargaining and Settling phases and we will need to consider the tactics and preparation which are appropriate for a Competitive negotiation.

Planning and Control must be re-emphasized.

And we conclude with two chapters equally applicable to Constructive or to Competitive Negotiations: the conduct of prolonged negotiations and the conduct of negotiations with people from different countries.

But first, the context of Competitive Negotiations.

CHAPTER 14

The Context of Competitive Negotiation

INTRODUCTION

This chapter sets the scene for our consideration of Competitive Negotiations. The chapter covers:

The attitudes of Competitive Negotiators
The key stages in Competitive Negotiators
Behaviour in the early stages.

ATTITUDES OF COMPETITIVE NEGOTIATORS

The competitive negotiator wants to win.

He wants to wrest advantage from the situation. And from the Other Party.

That is the crucial difference compared with the constructive negotiator. The latter wants to make the most of the situation in the joint interests of both parties. The competitive negotiator sees his task as being to wrest advantage from the others just as much as from the situation.

Here are some indications of his views.

First, his views of the situation:

(a)   It is a competitive world. I have to gain the upper edge.
(b)   I have to be quick and clever if I am to gain that advantage.
(c)   I must use winning tactics, and a bit of bluff is part of the fabric of negotiation.
(d)   I must not give way. I must get advantage from him before I relinquish anything.

And his views of the Other Party:

(a)   He is my opponent.
(b)   He will try to exploit me.
(c)   He is bound to try a few tricks on me.
(d)   He will want me to give him something before he gives me anything.

(e)   I must be wary of him.

The basic attitude of the competitive negotiator is to wrest advantage, both from the situation and from the Other Party.

THE KEY STAGES IN COMPETITIVE NEGOTIATION

Bargaining is the key in a competitive negotiation.

Bargaining is the phase in which we do our deals, in which we wheel and deal, in which we strive to gain the advantage. It is the phase in which we assert our shrewdness.

The bids which we have already made are very important too. They demarcate the area within which we shall conduct our bargaining.

For competitive negotiators, our preparation needs to focus towards winning the advantage in the crucial Bargaining phase. We therefore approach our negotiation with our minds well prepared to enter into those phases. Not so well prepared to enter into an exploration phase.

The balance of significance of the phases in the subject matter is shown in Figure 14.1.

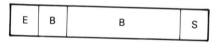

Fig. 14.1

BEHAVIOUR IN THE EARLY STAGES

We studied earlier a style of negotiation in which the thrust is to move matters so that the interests of the parties converge. A process in which the ice-breaking and the opening procedure create a supportive and trusting climate. Ripe for exploration of mutual interests and for the development of shared goals.

In competitive negotiations, those early stages take a different form. We will review that form in three sections:

1. Establishing the climate of a Competitive Negotiation.
2. The opening procedure.
3. Exploration in a Competitive Negotiation.

Establishing the climate

The Competitive Negotiator is of course concerned about the climate of a negotiation. He would even be glad to see the characteristics we suggested for a Constructive Negotiation: cordial, co-operative, brisk and businesslike. But he also wants to achieve other ends during the early ice-breaking phase. He wants to be finding more leverage.

Let us invent a couple of skilled Competitive Negotiators, Lew Barnes and Howard Lacy. In our first example, one of them (Lew) is going to meet Guy Smithson, our relatively inexperienced salesman.

Lew: "Well, hello Guy. Good to see you."

Guy: "Thank you. I am pleased to welcome you."

Lew: "Great. How's business with you?"

Guy: "Well, you know how things are. It's a difficult world nowadays and we're all in it together."

Lew: "Yes, certainly, and there's a lot of trouble around with people who are not doing their inspection fully; reject rates going up by leaps and bounds. I was with a company yesterday whose organization was rejecting 5 per cent more than 12 months ago. How much more are you getting returned nowadays?"

Lew has established that he can bargain very hard because of Guy's probable shortage of orders.

Having achieved this element of prospective leverage, he is quickly seeking to find out whether he can exert 'quality' leverage as well. He may well continue this form of exploration:

"And deliveries?"
"How about cash flow?"
"Exports?"

Lew is a good competitive negotiator. He might go thus far. Some would go even further, trying to establish some personal leverage, looking for the opponent's weaknesses in his financial status or his gambling habits. The extreme is of course the legend of the businessman lured to bed by a lovely lady, then next morning shown pictures of the performance. But that is an extreme which may be found in the world of politicians or spies, but not (to the extent of my knowledge) in the business world.

Lew is pretty ruthless in looking for his leverage but will not go so far as personal exploitation.

The ideal climate for a Competitive Negotiator might be Cordial, Cooperative, Brisk and Businesslike. But the form of the opening is more likely to be Competitive, Brisk and Businesslike, with less emphasis on the Cordial and Co-operative.

The opening procedure

As the negotiators sit down and move towards business, the Competitive Negotiator will handle the opening procedural phase in one of two ways.

Either he will brush it aside. This will leave the situation ambiguous. If one negotiator has a clear idea of the way he wants the meeting to unfold and the Other Party is not aware of it, then the others are disadvantaged. They find the problems of ambiguity and overload to which we referred earlier.

The counter-measure of the second party can, of course, be to prepare their own plan, which may also remain obscure. And so, each party can jostle to follow its own path. The result inevitably becomes constant squabbling on the procedural level through the main part of the negotiation.

Keeping one's agenda so obscure is a legitimate tactic, but one which I would not recommend.

Alternatively, the Competitive Negotiator may aim for a highly formalized agenda, one which is designed to give him distinctive advantage.

There is an oft-quoted formula for this sort of competitive agenda. We will be discussing it in Chapter 20—Preparation for Competitive Negotiations.

Exploration

In a Competitive Negotiation, the role of Exploration is to establish the sort of deal which could be to mutual advantage. The priority for the Competitors is not to explore but to move to the more significant (for them) phases of Bidding and Bargaining. It seems better to bargain over a ready-made package than to look for a mutually profitable venture.

Issues which might have been explored in a Constructive Negotiation may be left aside and only be brought up as additional evidence during the Bargaining phase.

When Charles Blackman and David Stanton negotiated the sale of some waste paper, they took care to include discussion of one another's priorities for length of contract, terms of settlement, etc., before making specific bids and offers.

Lew and Howard are likely to move into the Bidding Stage more quickly and to find that differences on length of contract and on terms of settlement emerge only during the bargaining phase.

In a Competitive Negotiation, the parties are anxious to reach the exciting phase of Bidding and Bargaining. They do not build foundations of trust, and are unlikely to search for creative possibilities and shared goals.

SUMMARY

1. The attitudes of competitive negotiators are to wrest advantage from the situation **and** from the Other Party.

2. The key stages of a competitive negotiation are Bidding and Bargaining. Earlier phases are less significant.
3. The established climate is likely to be more competitive and the procedural opening to be more formal or to be neglected.
4. Exploration, important as it is, is not of the same significance as later phases. The urge to bargain is paramount.

EXERCISE

1. What differences would there be in your approach to renting a room in a house in which you are to live and in buying text books from a student who was, last year, on the course which you will be studying this year?

FURTHER READING

Atkinson, G.G.M. (1975) *The Effective Negotiator*. London: Quest.
   Atkinson has written a very useful text about the skills of competitive negotiations conducted between unions and management. Much of what he says concerns the attitudes and objectives appropriate at different stages of a negotiation. His summary of the opening stage of negotiations is particularly relevant here. The basic objective is "to gain a maximum amount of information relating to Opponent's realistic settlement and even his fall back position, while revealing a minimum amount relating to your own." (p.88)
   This is, of course, exactly what Lew is starting to do.

Fisher, R. & Ury, W. (1983) *Getting to Yes: Negotiating Agreement Without Giving In*. London: Hutchinson.
   Discuss how to handle negotiators who adopt very aggressive positions and suggest some of the ways in which it may be possible, creatively to disagree (by dovetailing different interests).

CHAPTER 15
Bidding

INTRODUCTION

Bidding marks the beginning of the vital phase of a Competitive Negotiation. It is the phase in which the negotiating territory is staked out.

We need now to consider:

What bid should we make?
How should we put that bid?

CHOICE OF BID

The Competitive Negotiator, in search of the most advantageous position for himself, must aim high in order to wrest the most from the negotiation. Moreover, he anticipates that the Other Party will challenge him and that there will follow a crucial Bargaining period. In that period, his bid will be put under attack. Thus he has the further incentive to bid high: he needs room for manoeuvre.

There is a mathematical theory as to how high it is practical to aim. This theory is intellectually exciting (see for example Marsh 1984) but most commercial negotiators find it difficult or impossible to apply. They rely rather on that commercial experience which they have built up which enables them almost intuitively to recognize the appropriate bid.

High it must be. But it must also be defensible. If we aim too high, the Other Party will soon force us to make concessions. And once we are on the run, there is very little stopping.

The bidding will, of course, have to cover a range of variables. If we are bankers, then we need to put our bids in terms of how much, what security, what repayment, how long and what interest. If we are technologists, then in terms of specification, quality requirement, quality control, maintenance, servicing etc. If we are commercial people, then in terms of price, discount, delivery, settlement terms. Always, bids over a wide range of variables.

For continuing simplicity, we will continue to quote examples from the commercial world.

EXAMPLES

Let us consider how different negotiators might bid in a particular commercial situation.

A waste paper merchant calls to see a manufacturer who has waste paper to sell. Typically, the manufacturer is not desperately concerned: it is a by-product, a nuisance, something he wants to get rid of. He is no expert on the waste-paper market.

The buyer, on the other hand, is an expert. He is seeped in the waste paper trade. He knows that today he can sell on (to pulp mills) the waste he has bought and can realize £50 per ton. But that price is liable to go up or down quite dramatically. What's more, he has costs of transportation, sorting and warehousing of £15 per ton before he makes any profit.

Let us consider how different negotiators might approach this situation.

First, the inexperienced Guy Smithson as the seller, receiving the moderately experienced Tina Thorne. Tina would try to ensure suitable opening rituals, and then the dialogue might develop:

Guy: "Well, here's a sample of our waste paper. As you will see, it is good quality but we can make no further use of it, and we think it should be worth £50 a ton."

Tina: "Thank you for showing me the sample. It is, as you say, satisfactory quality. Before I could offer you a price, I would need further information, but I must say at the outset that £50 is far out of any possibility."

Guy: "But I heard of somebody who was getting £50."

Tina: "If you can promise amounts of 1,000 tons per week, sorted, baled and delivered to a mill 200 miles away, with heavy penalty clauses for any failures on your part, then I accept that you might recently have achieved as much as £50. You certainly wouldn't have got it 12 months ago, and you would be very lucky to get it again this week because the market is going downwards."

Guy: "Oh, I see. Well, in that case, how about £40?"

Tina: "Again, far too high."

Guy: "£30?"

Tina: "That's very difficult. There are a great deal of factors to be taken into account, and we'll need to spend a lot of time on those."

Guy: "Well, look, time is precious. Will it help us to settle if we agree to £25?"

He is on the run. He started by asking far too much, displaying his ignorance. Tina has ample opportunity now to move him to a settlement at £20 or £22.

99

If Sara Brady was selling and Martin McLean buying:

Martin:	"Well now, the price we can offer you is about £22."
Sara:	"About £22?"
Martin:	"Yes, that's the price we can offer you. You will appreciate that we have to collect it and sort it and bale it and warehouse it, as well as making enough to live on."
Sara:	"Now, just a minute. How much does it cost to sort it?"

Martin has made two basic mistakes.

First, he said "about £22". That word "about" is suicidal. What Sara hears is that he would take it at a price of something over £22 but she doesn't know how much more.

Nor will she ever find out. It doesn't matter that Martin will offer a higher price. And then maybe a still higher price. However far he goes, she will never be sure that she has exploited all she could of his "about" figure.

And having made that first mistake, he has gone on to try to justify his price. In doing so, he has invited Sara to challenge him on sorting costs.

Then on bailing costs.

Then on warehouse costs.

Then on profit margins.

*Maybe Sara would have done so anyway, but Martin makes a fool of himself by **inviting** her to do so.*

He didn't make his bid firmly. He offered unnecessary justification.

Charles Blackman is our constructive buyer. Given the scenario outlined at the start of these examples, Charles would have found out how much waste the seller had, what sort of contract he was looking for, long term or short term, the consistency of the quality and the nature of storage on site. He would also have given the seller a good sense of his own problems with the variation in prices at which he could sell on the waste he had bought. His later dialogue might go:

Charles:	"Thank you for the information. It is most helpful to know where we stand.
	"For this quality and a 12-month contract, 10 tons a week, I can offer you £28 a ton."
Seller:	"Oh, come, come. We were hoping for much more than that."
Charles:	"That's the price and we don't negotiate on price."
Seller:	"Please can you not think again? I was hoping for much more."
Charles:	"Well now, that's difficult unless you could accept a shorter contract—3 months."

The constructive negotiator does not set a smokescreen around his bids. Nor does he retract when he has put a firm and defensible bid. He does offer options to help the seller to "buy" a better price—but now we are moving into the next chapter, the field of Bargaining.

If Lew Barnes expected a settlement of £30, then he would bid £24.

He would put the bid with great firmness and conviction.

He and Howard Lacy would then have a very interesting bargaining session which, predictably, would end up with the price more or less at £30.

PRESENTATION OF BID

These examples are chosen for two reasons. The first is to underline the golden rule for Bidding. It is (for the seller) to make *the highest defensible bid*.

For the buyer, the corresponding phrase is of course *the lowest defensible offer*.

In the first example, Guy asked for a price which was unreasonable. Quickly, the buyer had him on the run. His price was not defensible. He had done damage by suggesting it.

That which is defensible is generally a matter of commercial judgement. It also depends on the style in which the negotiation is being conducted. A Competitive Negotiator will anticipate a need for later manoeuvring and will leave room for that manoeuvring in his bid. A Constructive Negotiator, better informed from his exploration and with a difference of attitude, will pitch his bid nearer to or even at the ultimate point of settlement.

That which is defensible is also related to differences in culture. Anybody selling in Eastern countries should anticipate a need to haggle which is anathema to most Western negotiators. In the one region, you leave an enormous amount of room for later bargaining. In the other, you pitch much nearer the final figure.

The examples also show the importance of skilled presentation of a bid. The use of the word "about" in one bid was damaging. In another example, putting the bid with inessential justification was an invitation to challenge.

Guidelines for the presentation of a bid are:

Clearly
Firmly
No justification

When you receive a bid from the Other Party, you should make quite

101

sure that you know what that bid represents. Get clear: does it include tax? Transport? Insurance? What precisely does it cover?

Distinguish these questions for clarification from questions for justification until you reach the Bargaining phase.

Finally, there is a question of whether it pays to be the opening bidder. In most circumstances the question is axiomatic. If I am being sold a car, then I expect the seller to make the first bid. He is the expert. If, on the other hand, I am a manufacturer selling waste paper, then I expect the buyer to make the first bid. He is the expert.

In the rare cases when it is not obvious who should first offer a bid, there is some advantage in each direction. The opening bidder sets the expectations—the first figure announced is very powerful. But the respondent then has time to modify his own thinking and to pitch his first offer in the light of the Other Party's bid. The relative merits of the two strategies are well balanced.

SUMMARY

1. Choose the highest defensible bid. If buying, the lowest defensible offer.
2. Put it:

> Firmly
> Clearly
> Without justification

3. Constructive negotiators pitch their initial bids nearer to the expected final settlement.
4. Competitive negotiators leave more room for manoeuvre.
5. Respond to any bid by first getting clarification, not yet justification.

EXERCISE

1. You are selling, privately, a 10-year old car which you have maintained yourself. It is in impeccable condition both mechanically and in the bodywork and is taxed, insured and MOT'd for 6 months. A friend of yours in the motor trade has told you that the trade price according to Glass's Guide (the bible of the secondhand motor trade) is:

trade price buying—£675.
trade price selling—£1175.

What would be your highest defensible price at which to offer the car?
If you were buying the car, at what figure would you bid?

FURTHER READING

Atkinson, G.G.M. (1975) *The Effective Negotiator*. London: Quest.
Gives a useful and non-mathematical discussion of where to pitch the initial bid. Atkinson tries to capture the spirit of some of the formal analyses of bargaining power, but in a form which can be used. His discussion of bidding is then linked to his discussion of bargaining power. This is a sensible move to make, although Atkinson does little more than outline some of the basic ideas.

Hawkins, K. (1979) *A Handbook of Industrial Relations Practice*. London: Kogan Page.
Shows the importance of basing initial offers on a thorough analysis of what the other side wants. The analysis shows very clearly that whilst negotiation is different from other forms of argument it is not just haggling. Any bid that is made will have to be justified. Whether it can be justified, and how it can be justified, are important elements of negotiation power. This point is amplified in
Morley, I.E. & Stephenson, G.M. (1977) *The Social Psychology of Bargaining*. London: George Allen & Unwin.
Hawkins also points out one important reason for clarifying any proposal put forward by the other side, finding out what exactly is involved. It is to make it more difficult for the other side to change the nature of their claim as negotiations proceed.

Marsh, P.D.V. (1984) *Contract Negotiation Handbook*. Aldershot: Gower Press.
Gives a detailed treatment of bidding based on formal economic models of concession making. The treatment is the best of its kind that I have read. However, the trend in bargaining theory is away from models of this kind. Many people feel that they give a spurious idea of precision, and that they are, in any case, too difficult to use.

Video Arts (1985). *So You Think You Can Sell?* London: Methuen.
Gives an excellent example of a negotiator who has lost control, rather in the way that Martin (see p. 100) has lost control in this chapter.

Winkler, J. (1981) *Bargaining for Results*. London: Heinemann.
There are two related sides to Martin's dilemma. The first is, do not give people unnecessary opportunities to ask questions you do not want to answer. The other side of the coin, which Winkler discusses, is do not ask them a question if you know you are not going to like their answer.

CHAPTER 16
Bargaining: Part 1

INTRODUCTION

In this book as a whole we are breaking the treatment of the subject matter into Exploration, Bidding, Bargaining and Settling.

We now come to the phase of Bargaining. Important as this subject is in any negotiation, it is particularly important within a competitive negotiation. We are therefore devoting two chapters to Bargaining, with the special benefit that the second of the chapters is contributed by a specialist author on the subject. In a third chapter, we will reinforce the two on Bargaining with one on Competitive Tactics.

In this first chapter on Bargaining, the subject will be divided into four main sections:

1. Bargaining Strategies.
2. Defining the Bargaining Ground.
3. The Human Element.
4. Concession Patterns.

BARGAINING STRATEGIES

As a general rule, be positive during the Bargaining phase. There are bound to be some differences between that which one party offers, and that which the other wants. If that gap is seen as a massive rift, then it becomes an insurmountable obstacle to achieving a deal. If, on the other hand, it is seen as a challenge to be overcome, then there is much higher hope of settlement.

Compare
That's a hell of a difference!
That's quite a gap for us to overcome.

There is a distinction between a strategy of Chip-Away and one of Counter Offer. During the Bidding phase, one party has made a bid. The other can respond by chipping away, bit by bit, trying to reduce a bid. Or, from the other side, bit by bit trying to get an increased offer.

"£100,000? That's far too much. You'll have to come down."

The alternative is to counter-offer.

"100,000? That's very much more than we had contemplated. Our expectation was £80,000."

The chip-away strategy is a strong and aggressive strategy. It leaves the Other Party uncertain and disoriented about what he may yet have to do. It is a tactic beloved of aggressive negotiators and is suitable for those in a strong negotiating position. The buyer in a buyer's market. The monopsonist when there are many competing suppliers. The technologist with a unique product. Unless you are in a strong position, however, beware of this approach. It may drive away people with whom you could well have done good business.

The counter offer is a more constructive strategy. It is also the one which should be sought by negotiators defending against aggressive opponents.

Patience is a virtue in bargaining. There are always likely to be differences of view, and however skilled the negotiators those differences may take time to reduce. The impatient negotiator is likely to try to rush forward. He will not only make himself frustrated if he does so; he will also be vulnerable. He will be inclined to offer concessions which the more patient party will absorb without full recompense.

The Scandinavians have a concept of "Ripeness". They perceive that both situations and people change and develop. There comes a time when they are ripe for some new movement.

They are patient people. They do not try either to pluck fruit or to force the progress of bargaining until the time is ripe.

Use recesses. Take plenty of breaks during Bargaining. Both you and the Other Party need time to reconsider as you make progress, suddenly discover fresh obstacles to be overcome and move nearer your goal and need new strategies for the next phase.

A break also revives the energy which the negotiators have in the negotiating room. It helps to overcome that deterioration of energy which invariably takes place during the conduct of any negotiation.

Here are two examples of different approaches to Bargaining Strategy. They assume that one person has a truck which he is not using much. Another is in need of a similar truck.

First Martin and Guy.

Guy: "Well, I'll give you £12,000 for it."
Martin: "£12,000? No, that's quite inadequate. You'll have to go up
          a long way from that."

Guy: "Well, that seems to me to be a fair price and one that you'll be lucky to get. That is a fair offer."

Martin: "Well, it's nowhere near enough."

Guy: "All right, for friendship's sake, I'll stretch a point, how about £12,500?"

Martin went on trying to chip-away at Guy's bid. Guy kept giving small concessions until both grew impatient.

Consider how other negotiators might have tackled the same situation.

Lew: "Thank you very much for putting me in the picture about the truck and its present condition. On that evidence, I can offer you £12,000 for it."

Tina: "£12,000? That's a great surprise. I was expecting very much more."

Lew: "I'm sorry to hear that. Can you give me any indication of what was in your thinking?"

Tina: "Frankly, my expectation was nearer to £17,000."

Lew: "Well, as you said a few minutes ago, it's in my interests to have the truck at work, and it's in your interests to have a workable truck. There is quite a gap for us to bridge between £12,000 and £17,000. May I suggest that we go away and think about ways to come closer to one another? Maybe I could call on you again this afternoon?"

These negotiators are positive. Tina's immediate reaction was to chip-away, but she responded to Lew's request for an "indication" with a counter offer. They didn't rush their fences. When difficulties loomed, they took a recess. They have achieved better hope of making progress.

To summarize: key elements to Bargaining strategy are
                Be positive.
                Choose between chip-away and counter-offer.
                Be patient
                Use breaks.

DEFINING THE BARGAINING GROUND

First, define the issues to be confronted during the Bargaining phase. Both the hard issues, the ones which are easy to quantify, price, delivery, terms, specifications and so on. And the soft issues, the less precise ones such as performance guarantees, the importance of service, quality issues, performance guarantees.

Unless you have the issues clear in your own thinking, you will find that you are failing to get some advantages you might have earned whilst unwittingly surrendering concessions.

Distinguish between vertical and lateral negotiations.

The vertical negotiator will start discussing prices and go right on discussing prices into a great deal of depth. Then progress to deep-diving on the next issue.

The lateral negotiator will try to keep matters on a broad front. To make limited progress on price and on quality and delivery and a dozen other variables.

Then another limited move on the broad front.

The vertical strategy is a tough one, used by strong parties to erode the other's position. The lateral strategy offers better prospects of trading concessions and of face-saving—two important aspects of Bargaining to be discussed later in this chapter.

Prioritize. Make up your mind which are the more important issues for you and which the less important. Then try to establish what are the Other Party's priorities: what really matters to him and what is less significant.

If delivery is critical for you whereas settlement terms are critical for him then you can do a deal to your mutual advantage. You can both find a way of slicing the cake to your own tastes.

Ask for hints and indications.

In the truck example above, Martin used a chip-away strategy and Guy let him get away with it. Lew, on the other hand, asked for an indication of Tina's thinking and achieved a better understanding from which to make progress.

To summarize, in defining the Bargaining ground

   Determine whether to approach vertically or laterally
   Establish respective priorities
   Seek for hints and indications.

THE HUMAN ELEMENT

The other negotiator is a person. He wants to do a good job and he needs to achieve a deal which will be satisfactory. Satisfactory for his company and satisfactory for him.

Each negotiator must stick firmly to his ground. He must be doing all he can to achieve the best possible result for his own side.

Without in any way yielding on the essential need to do a good job for your own side, recognize that the other person has the same need. Find ways which will enable him to take home a deal which he can sell to his management and receive their approval.

Do check on his opinion. Just think of the way you would respond to my saying: "It would be helpful for you to buy a shower. It would enable you to be much fitter. You would feel much better if you had a cold shower every morning."

Contrast the alternative approach.
"Are you interested in keeping fit?"
"In what ways will a shower help you?"

Any time somebody tries to tell me what I think or what I ought to think I get furious. It does not matter how hard they have tried to think out what would be in my interests. My interests are my affair and I don't like people who try to take over my territory.

If somebody asks me what are my interests, then they both stimulate me to think about the question and they learn from my replies.

Help to save face.

You have argued hard for the outcome which would be ideal for your side. He has argued equally hard for his side. It is difficult for either of you to concede, even when you know that the time is ripe.

It is not only the interests of each side that is at stake: it is also the "face" of each negotiator. His self-image and the respect which he thinks he has with the Other Party.

A head-on collision creates a situation where prestige is at risk. The solution is to keep it fluid. Introduce another variable to take tension out of the conflict.

Don't let the argument become concentrated on price alone. Introduce some other variable which will take the tension out of the situation.

Normally, try to bargain laterally, so that several variables will be under consideration at the same time. This enables you to handle the need to move on price in conjunction with the opportunity to move at the same time on quantity and delivery, or whatever.

If you are running short of real issues to take the heat out of the situation, then be inventive. Find one.

"Well, then the situation seems to be that we have to bridge a gap between £80,000 and £100,000, but before we try to do this, would it help if we discussed the risk involved?"

You will find that even if you have invented a reason which is not of much validity, it is still a catalyst enabling both parties to move forward without the same sense of loss of face.

Keep it fluid, but not too fluid. If negotiators are handling, say, three variables at one time, they can squeeze those variables until a shape is achieved which is mutually acceptable.

But if you try to squeeze half a dozen variables at one time, then it is too much for your overloaded brain.

My mind can handle price, delivery and terms at one and the same time.

If, at the same time, you ask it to permutate not only price, delivery and terms, but performance guarantees and training specifications and colour requirements and a few other things, you would have got me overloaded. I cannot cope.

To summarize: remember that he is a person and he is as concerned as you to go back with a satisfactory report. With minimum prejudice to your own needs, find how best to satisfy his needs.

Check his opinion; avoid telling him what it should be.

Ask the questions which will help you both to recognize his interests.

Help him to save face.

Keep it fluid.

Not too fluid. Do not let it get ambiguous.

CONCESSION PATTERNS

In any negotiation where there is a difference of bids there must be some making of concessions. There are three golden rules for this phase. They are:

Trade concessions.
Move at a measured pace.
Avert impasses.

First, trade concessions. The skilled negotiator never concedes on "this" without a corresponding concession from the Other Party on "that". He uses "this" to buy "that"—he does not just give it away.

Second, he moves at a measured pace. When there is a difference of opinion, he does not expect that everything will be sorted out in one session. He expects that the two parties will gradually move closer together, step by step, through a succession of intriguing meetings.

He plans each potential concession that he will have to make and the corresponding concession he will expect from the Other Party at the same time. Here is an illustration of concessions planned and anticipated in three stages. The parties are predicted to come to a settlement at a point between their original bids, moving at a measured pace.

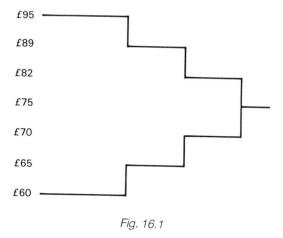

Fig. 16.1

He has his own theories about the sizes of the steps in that concession pattern. Should the first step be larger or smaller than the second, the third, and what about the length of time between each successive concession? There is much literature on this subject but no definitive theory.

Third, the skilled negotiator is wary of reaching an impasse. As he sees one looming, however distantly, he will take a recess and look for means to avoid it. He will be diligent in searching for face-saving formulae, for introducing new variables, for keeping things fluid.

Let us go back to Lew and Tina discussing the truck. We left them as they summarized that a deal would be in their joint interest and there was a gap between £12,000 and £17,000 for them to overcome.

When Martin and Guy were faced with the problem, they failed to handle the bargaining to mutual satisfaction and they did not reach a deal. Let us consider how Lew and Tina might have developed the discussion.

Tina: "So we had a mutual desire to find ways of using the truck. The major problem to be overcome was the difference on price. We have to find ways to bridge a gap between £12,000 and £17,000."

Lew: "'Yes, I agree exactly. That's what we have to achieve today. Let's start by checking what new thinking we have each brought to the discussion."

Tina: "Well, I was wondering whether we might be able to come closer together if we consider how we could stage payments. How about you?"

Lew: "Interesting. My thinking was on the lines that I'm not using the truck much now but may need it again in 2 or 3 years' time. I was wondering if we might build in a re-purchase option?"

Tina: "That sounds interesting—could you go into it a little further?"

Lew: "Well, I had been thinking of £17,000 as a price for the truck. It would help me if you would give me an option to buy it back, say, in 2 years' time."

Tina: "I see that, but how would we deal with the price for that re-purchase?"

Lew: "Well, we could agree that here and now."

Tina: "Are you suggesting, then, something like a price of £14,000 with a three year re-purchase option at £6,000?"

Lew: "Those are not the figures I had in mind, but that's certainly the principle of it."

Tina: "What are the figures you had in mind, then?"

Lew: "You mean that, in principle, that's the sort of arrangement you can tolerate?"

Tina: "Yes, I think that's very constructive provided the figures are right."

Lew: "I was thinking of dropping the price from £17,000 to £15,000 if you would give me re-purchase in two years for £5,000."

Tina: "That's a bit difficult for me, I'm afraid. With figures of £15,000 and £6,000 I'd be looking for a 4-year deal."

And now the two negotiators have a comfortably fluid position to squeeze. They have the purchase price, the date of re-purchase and the price of re-purchase.

There are strong hopes that they will find ways of squeezing these issues to their mutual satisfaction. And they have in reserve the option to look at staged payments as another possible avenue to bring them together.

They are trading concessions, moving at a measured pace and avoiding any impasse.

SUMMARY

1. Bargaining is important in most negotiations and is the vital phase of competitive negotiations.
2. Basic strategy for this phase is:

   > Be positive
   > Decide on chip-away or counter offer.
   > Be patient.
   > Use breaks.

111

3. Define the Bargaining ground.

> Define the issues
> Distinguish vertical from lateral.
> Prioritize.
> Seek for hints and indications.

4. The human element: with minimum prejudice to your own need for a good deal, remember that he too is a person who needs to take home a satisfactory deal.

> Check his opinion, do not force yours on him, ask him for his.
> Keep it fluid.
> Not too fluid.

5. In making concessions:

> Trade concessions, do not give them away.
> Move at a measured pace.
> Avoid impasses.

EXERCISE

1. In the example of buying/selling a car at the end of Chapter 15, what concessions would you be able to trade? How would these concessions be reflected in the price?

FURTHER READING

Morley, I.E. (1987) Negotiation and Bargaining. In Hargie, O. (ed.) *A Handbook of Communication Skills*. London: Croom Helm.

Morley, I.E. (1981) Negotiating and Bargaining. In Argyle, M. (ed.) *Social Skills and Work*. London: Methuen.
Both the above texts underscore Bill Scott's point that in various ways skilled negotiators will help their opponents. Examples from Bill's chapter include: "Find ways which will enable him to take home a deal which he can sell to his management and receive their approval for". "Help save face." Other examples are given in Morley's writing. Thus, models which liken negotiation to warfare (even guerrilla warfare) tell only part of the story.

Pruitt, D.G. (1981) *Negotiation Behavior*. New York: Academic Press.
Pruitt summarizes what has been learned about the dynamics of concession-making from the results of experimental negotiations, and from some field studies. Some attention is given to horizontal and to vertical strategies. It is important to note, however, that one of the jobs Bill Scott is trying to do is to show that there is more to negotiation than just concession-making. Some

writers have argued that the main problem is to find a "formula" which justifies any deal in terms of the kinds of things which have been done in the past, and will be done in the future. The classic statement of this position is, perhaps:

Zartman, I.W. (1977) Negotiation as a Joint Decision Process. *Journal of Conflict Resolution* **21**, 619–38. This paper has been reprinted in Zartman, I.W. (ed.) *The Negotiation Process*. Beverly Hills: Sage.

Kniveton, B.K. & Towers, B. (1978) *Training for Negotiation: A Guide for Management and Employee Relations*. London: Business Books.

This is a very readable introduction to some of the skills of negotiation. As the title suggests, the book tries to identify the kinds of skills which it is important to develop in training courses on negotiation. There is a very interesting comparison of the vertical and horizontal approaches to bargaining, which is well worth reading.

CHAPTER 17

Bargaining: Part 2

This is the second of two chapters on the bargaining phase of a negotiation. It has been contributed by John Winkler, an expert on bargaining, and author of *Bargaining for Results*.

PRICE BARGAINING TACTICS

If he wants a better price then give him one.

Provided he gives you a better order.

Practically all big deals are complex, 'multi-faceted'. Price is only one of the issues to be agreed, but it is often the central issue around which the rest of the deal revolves. So we have to look at the rest of the deal. There are hundreds of ways for buyers to get your price down, without complaining about your price. What they do is to demand that your service goes up.

Here is how to get what you want out of a complex deal. Remember you are not fighting a battle, you are working towards a solution which is good for both companies—yours and his. That's the first rule. The second is to know what you want, and be able to have a good guess at what he wants. Next, you must decide whether you are going to bundle up all that you want in a package, or break it up into separate bits. Then you go for the exchange.

COLLABORATION IS THE SOURCE OF A GOOD DEAL

You cannot go in strong with your demands on the other man if he does not want what you offer. The unique properties of your offer must be stressed, and be shown to be important to him. In terms of the value for money you propose to him, your offer must be a veritable star in a wilderness of competition. He will not show you that he is excited by what you are offering; this is part of his ritual in keeping your expectations pressed down.

But when you reach the stage where both of you are inclined to do business with each other, then search for joint benefits in the deal. Many times, deals are constructed as one-way moves—the gains of one side are paid for by the other side. If the buyer gets your price down and nothing else happens, then he has saved himself money, at your expense.

You need to escape from this situation of one-way gains and losses. You need to move into the area where both of you can do better.

For example, he might get your price down. But in exchange he agrees to pick up the product from your warehouse and to pay you within 7 days. Alternatively, you suggest a way of manufacturing for him in large batches to suit your production, and with joint storage until he calls off the product, then you can give him a really special price. Alternatively, instead of his taking supplies from three different companies, you might show him the advantage of taking 80 per cent of his requirement from you which will earn him the maximum quantity discount. This leaves 20 per cent to another supplier which provides him with the security of supplies he needs.

The first principle of exchange is to search for collaboration, rather than to engage in conflict.

The best deal is a deal with adequate profit for both sides.

SETTING THE OBJECTIVES

You must know what you want from him and you must put this up against what you think he wants from you. List all the things you offer him, together with the price you want. Rank them in order of importance to you—certain things you must have, such as standard specification, prompt payment, or your price objective. In addition, there are things you would like to have such as a much bigger volume order. And you would like to try for a higher price. Perhaps you would also like to get cash up front. It's not always possible, but you have to trade in the demand somehow. In dealing, if you don't trade it in and ask for it, then you certainly will not get it.

Then set out his priorities: what you think he will demand from you. What must he have, what do you think he would like to have? He is going to try to get it all, if he can, and you must work out what you think he will settle for at base, and what you think he will try on.

Break up what you offer into bits. You can agree to it after an argument, in exchange for something from him. If you give free servicing and maintenance, then separate this. Ask him if he wants it. If he does, then what can he give you back?

There may be bits in your package that you normally take for granted and offer to everyone. There may also be other things which you can do for him and which he wants once you mention them to him. Many of these things will cost you only a little. But they might be of considerable importance to him.

Many of the things you want from them, and many of the things they

115

want from you, will be unable to be quantified. You might want efficient order processing and few last-minute rushes. They might want from you absolute reliability. If you say you are going to do something, then you must be relied upon to do it.

These things cannot be quantified. But they can be listed and traded into the package. You can offer reliability, if perhaps you offer yourself personally to look after their business. Would they want that? (If you have done the deal well, then they will want that.) You are willing to handle their business personally, but they must give you direct access to their people and keep to a regular plan for meetings. Their order office must work smoothly with yours and so on.

Pricing for results

1. Objective:
   Like to have
   Must have
   Do not want
2. Priorities
3. What will he want?
4. What can he give us in exchange?
5. What concessions are of **most value** to him and of **least cost** to us?

BUNCHING OR BREAKING

You know all the things you want from him, and can guess at the things he wants from you. You will have to decide now whether to bunch or break.

Bunching is where you bundle together in a package all the things you want from him, put them all up front and tell him your offer. You try and secure agreement on the lot. You can bunch elements of the deal together without putting in the whole lot.

Or you can break up the deal into small bits and trade them one by one. You secure agreement on each principal bit before you move on. But you cannot bunch things together unless the other person understands all the components you are offering.

Very often, whether you should bunch or break is clear from the situation. If he is generally ignorant about what you propose, then you must take him through it bit by bit.

But he also can bunch or break up his demands upon you. Once you have told him of your offer, he can think about it a bit and then come at you with a complete package which includes everything that he wants, and he can then offer you a price which seems to be "take it or leave it". What should you do? You should separate it and break it up into bits as far as you can. Take the main item, and press him precisely on his requirements there. Then take the next. Cost each item separately as you go, and your costing will now show a higher price than he has offered you. This is the area where you must trade. If he won't raise his price to you, then you must leave something out of the package which he wants. That's dealing.

A buyer will use this technique if he knows the field very well, or if he wants to frighten you out of making a high price demand.

Most buyers do not know the limit of all the concessions they can get. They test out each supplier in turn. They try and secure a general commitment from the salesman on the issue of price, without themselves being committed to buying at that price. They then go in with their big demand first, and try to get the salesman to agree to that. Then they move in with their next, and so on down the list.

Having committed himself on price, but not having secured the buyer's agreement to buy, the salesman finds himself being chipped away, bit by bit, until all his discretion to offer extra services or to make price reductions has been taken away from him, until finally he says "no".

The tactic to use here is again the opposite one. If they are bunching, you should break it up: if they are breaking, then you should bunch your side of the deal. Do not become committed to your lowest price early on. Find out what else they want in the deal first. Explain that you can only price the deal when you know all that they want from you. Then you bunch all their demands together and price the whole package.

The strategies of breaking and bunching do not solve all the problems of dealing with skilled buyers. But they allow you to lose less often.

Finally, you will get to a situation where you are going to exchange the things they want from you for the things you want from them. You will be able to see the items which link together nicely. Like goes with like for the most part; and high value goes with high value. Most of the linking issues will be obvious. If they want you to waive your minimum order requirement for product A, then they will have to give you a full vehicle delivery. Could their orders on A be linked to a higher volume deal on B which would make up the load? If they want to put in their own quality control inspectors on your production line, then they will have to guarantee by contract to take the whole volume of output on that line, and so on. This is the lovely, creative part of dealing. Before you can get to it, however, you must both want something from each other and your respective power must be more or less equalized. If one of you does not want the other, then there is no point in looking for these exchanges.

Collaborative bargaining: Not conflict bargaining
Set your objectives: Don't play it as it comes
Sort out the bits you want: Don't do all the giving
If he breaks up his demands: You bunch them
If he bunches his demands: You break them
If you . . . then we . . . : Don't give it away

HOW TO TIE STRINGS

Be careful how you link issues together. If you are going to make a concession to them on price or discount, be careful to ensure that something comes back the other way. Otherwise you will be left offering them the lower price and forgetting to hook it up to something. The way to do this is to start with the two magic words "If you . . . ". When you are linking issues, if you get into the habit of putting up front these two words, followed by what you want from them, you have then made a condition on what you are going to give them. You can then go on in the last part of the sentence to say "Then we . . . ".

"If you can get the order to us by Monday, confirmed in writing, then we can get it to you for your Thursday production, guaranteed." "If you introduce this question to your colleagues on the main board, so that the whole group business which is worth £250,000 a year comes to us, then we will give your own company an extra rebate of 1.5 per cent on the business we do together." "If you cut down the branch of your tree which overhangs our kitchen window, then we'll stop our cat from terrorizing your budgerigar." "If you hand over your wallet, then I'll put this gun away."

SUMMARY

The best deals are those with profit to both sides. Deals where one side loses are unhealthy and rarely stick. So it pays to work towards collaboration where both sides can win more of what they want. But in any deal there will always be an element of one side seeking to gain an advantage at the expense of the other side. Getting a supplier to reduce his price and offering nothing extra in exchange is one such means most frequently used by buyers. They may carry out a plan to do this quite deviously, and it pays to be on guard most of the time to avoid being caught in a buyer's trap.

A difficult buyer is not usually one who sounds pugnacious or makes extreme demands. His manner, on the contrary, might be warm and affiliative, seeking to relax the sales executive. Typically, he will seek to anchor down the seller's price early in the conversation.

He might argue fiercely over this, and then move on to other matters, seeking to come back to the price later. His objective is to secure a commitment from the salesman without himself making a commitment to buy. It can happen that he might not argue too fiercely over the price, having anchored it down, because his principal objective might be to secure some other large concession as part of the package he wants. The value of the concession might be more than he can expect to obtain on price, so he might soften his price argument and introduce his big demand early.

Throughout all of this, it is important for the seller to avoid being caught in the trap of granting all the concessions one way. The settler should have a list of what he wants and should match this against his thoughts about what the customer might want. Breaking up the deal into component bits is a very important part of the dealing process. Many sellers become bored with the prospect of a long haggle over the detail, and try to clear up all the outstanding issues in a bundle. They concede the small things in the deal without thinking. Then they approach the end of the conversation to find that they have given away all of the cards they hold, and the buyer still has not committed himself to doing the deal. It is a major error of selling strategy and one to be avoided at all costs.

To avoid it, simply do not name the price up front. You can float an idea of it if you like, but leave yourself plenty of room. Every time he makes another demand upon you, then you must cost it out loud. When he has exhausted all his demands then you can add up the individual costs of what he wants from you. The total of all these costs will be much higher than the price you would have quoted him firmly at the start. Now you are free to give him this total price, and then deal from there.

Assess in advance what he is likely to want. Be careful to tie the strings to any deal you offer him. Make your offer conditional upon his doing something for you in return.

EXERCISES

1. If you were the college authorities in Exercise 2 (Chapter 13) would you bunch or break the negotiation?
2. What unquantifiable items can the Students' Union representatives offer when negotiating in Exercise 2?

FURTHER READING

Winkler, J. (1981) *Bargaining for Results*. London: Heinemann.
    Provides elaboration and extension of the points made in this chapter.

Winkler, J. (1983) *Pricing for Results*. London: Heinemann.

CHAPTER 18
Competitive Tactics

INTRODUCTION

The kernel of competitive negotiating is the Bargaining phase. The skilled negotiator prepares himself for that phase and during it is likely to use a range of special tactics. We shall deal with the preparation in Chapter 20. First, this chapter on Competitive Tactics.

The topic is one which has been the subject of much writing. In this chapter, we discuss only a selection of the most common tactics.

The first is a particular pattern for the agenda for a Bargaining phase. There is an assumption that the competitive negotiator will develop this phase in a manner described (in Chapter 16) as vertical. He is then recommended to establish the agenda in the sequence:

(a)   An easy issue: one on which he will give a little.
(b)   A second easy issue: one on which he will expect to get a little.
(c)   The toughest issue.

Subsequent issues in decreasing orders of toughness.

The thinking behind this sequence is that on Item (a), the negotiator can show what a reasonable person he is without having to give way on something important. He next establishes the style in which the Other Party is going to negotiate. By the time he comes to the important issues, this is supposed to have established that he is a reasonable person, and he knows how to style his negotiation.

This is consistent advice of many authorities for the agenda of a competitive negotiation.

"Lack of authority" is a tactic used by many negotiators.

If the Other Party is pushing you heavily for a concession, you plead lack of authority. You say you are not allowed to go that far. But of course you are well aware that other people may try this on you. So right at the beginning of every negotiation, you should ask "Are you authorized to settle this matter?" This may not stop him later saying that he has not the authority, but you are in a stronger position.

In much the same bag are questions of legal limits and of local customs.

The unscrupulous negotiator may cite either as part of his campaign to exert leverage. This device can be readily used in international negotiations because neither party can be expert in the detailed commercial laws or customs of the other's country.

Personally, I do not believe in these devices. I have enough difficulty coping with the demands of any type of negotiation without making it unnecessarily complicated. I want to earn a reputation for credibility, not to confuse the pattern with misleading devices.

Nevertheless, I recognize that other people adopt tough tactics and I have to be prepared for them.

Here are some other examples:

Straw Issues: Make mountains out of molehills. Seize on any trivial item and argue like mad on this item. Exhaust the other person. Then bring up your mountainous requirement. Trade your concessions on the molehill for his concession on the mountain.

"All I have got is 60 per cent of the price." This may be a true statement, in which case it helps constructive negotiators to search for what possibilities there would be with only 60 per cent.

On the other hand, it may not be true. It may be another device designed to mislead the Other Party. As such, it may gain short-term advantage at the expense of long-term credibility.

Body Language: Many competent authorities argue that you should pay great attention to people's faces, postures, gestures and body language. They say that you can tell whether they are bluffing or not by their body language.

There are some signs which are blatantly obvious. If a negotiator pushes back his chair and folds his arms, he is showing lack of interest.

There are other signs which are not so obvious. If he pulls his ear, is it because his ear is itching or is it because he does not want to hear what you are saying? There is a wealth of enlightening literature on this subject. (See Further Reading.)

My own experience is that I am short of energy in any negotiation. I am too short of energy to be able to devote some of it to studying signs which I will anyway have difficulty in interpreting.

At the extreme, some authorities tell negotiators to observe "blink rate". The frequency with which a negotiator blinks is said to be an indication of his stress level and his credibility. When I have tried to study this blink rate, I have found that it absorbs all my energy: I have not even heard the words that the other person is speaking.

Nor, amongst thousands of experienced negotiators with whom I have worked, have I yet found one who regularly practises reading of body language. They find it an intriguing subject, but not very practical.

Lubrication. Of course you are the sort of person who would not contemplate bribery, any more than I would.

So both of us lose dozens of deals we should make. It is no use going to half the countries in the world unless we are prepared to operate within the expected modus operandi.

It is the sort of thing you and I not only would not do. It is also the sort of thing which neither of us could do competently.

So what we have to do is to find somebody who will do the job for us. We have to find an agent who will work on a percentage and who will do the necessary for us out of his percentage.

But this is not as easy as it sounds. If you had recently gone to some African country, you would have found that it was essential to have an agent who was well-connected in the ruling tribe. In some countries where there is heavy political risk, the need is not to work with the present ruling tribe—they will be supplanted and their communications discarded before you can show the results of your negotiations. You need to guess who will next be in power and to have a proposition ready developed to suit their tastes.

Whichever it may be, it is essential for you to have an agent with the right connections and with skills in local customs including lubrication.

It used to be simple to find people claiming that they had the expertise and contacts. Business class hotels were crowded with people claiming to be the President's brother-in-law. You were then faced with the problem of deciding amongst all these aspirant brothers-in-law.

The only way round this problem—and it is a problem you are going to find today in many countries—is to go to the Commercial Section of your Embassy. They will advise you with the greatest strength and sincerity that you must not in any circumstances become involved in bribery, and without batting an eyelid give you the name and address of the President's real brother-in-law.

Changing the Shape of the Deal. When you have argued for weeks over the price of terms for buying a liner and the Other Party is totally exhausted, shift the ground. Talk about half a dozen tugs instead.

Go Upstairs. When it is too tough, get your boss to ring his boss.

The "Yes, but . . . " Tactic. This is a tactic beloved by sales-trainers and is in fact counter-productive. The thought is that every time the other chap bids on something you nod your head and say "yes . . . yes . . . yes . . .". Then you add "but . . . " and sweep in with your own overpowering arguments.

The reason that it is counter-productive is that the other chap recognizes this word "but" as disagreement, and he does not like being "butted".

The winning tactic is "Yes, and . . . .".

This is a tactic taught me by Dr Sven Soderberg. Sven sits capably in his negotiator's chair, smiling benignly, regularly saying "yes, and . . . " and coming up with the most positive, supportive comments for what the other people are talking about. He wins friends and influences people and makes deals, and I wish I could emulate him.

"That was an understanding not an agreement." This is a tactic that you will find especially in Bulgaria. You have an exhausting day. But at last you get away from it with an agreement on colour: you can have blue ones provided you agree to pay an extra 5 pence each.

Tomorrow they are back with you in the negotiating room talking about pink ones. Now this is very difficult for you because yesterday you gained only the colour concession. It was an exhausting day, and you'd had to concede 5 pence. And so you calmly point out that yesterday we agreed on blue, to which the Bulgarians reply, "Ah, that was an understanding not an agreement".

Whilst in Bulgaria, there is another device that you will find used there as well as in universities throughout the world. This is *The Minutes*. You go home exhausted tonight from all the negotiating you have been doing. You come back tomorrow morning and the Bulgarians start the day most courteously by handing you the minutes of yesterday's discussion. You are impressed with this efficiency and of course you have no time to digest the minutes, let alone check or challenge the detail of them.

When you get back home three weeks later, you discover that the full minutes show that you have agreed to some deal that you cannot remember having heard of. This is the tactic called "the Minutes".

"This price is not negotiable." This is a tactic I use. I never negotiate on price and I make this clear from the outset. Most people respect me for this, but bureaucrats have a habit of saying: "We don't have that much in the budget". This is taken to be a crushing argument, but I have discovered that there is a simple response which works wonders. It is: "I am very sorry to hear that. Will you please look for another budget".

I never negotiate on price. But I am not totally stupid: I am prepared to negotiate on discounts.

Be careless from time to time. Leave odd papers lying around which the Other Party might gracelessly pick up and look at after you have left.

Howard, our competitive salesman, is an expert on this tactic. He even prepares occasional memos specially to leave lying around. If, for example, he foresees that the Other Party is going to be very tough on delivery, he will have in his brief case a memo from his Sales Director. This will include the statement that under no circumstances must he drop below some prescribed delivery. That memo, left carelessly on the table at the end of the day's negotiations, can have a profound effect on his hosts.

Good Guy/Bad Guy Tactic. Take somebody else with you to your next negotiation, a nice reasonable chap. Yourself, behave normally. Lose your temper, get up and walk out. Leaving the good guy to apologize for your normal boorishness. The other people will recognize him for the nice chap he really is and will feel so sorry for him having to work with you that they will now offer a much better deal than you could ever have got.

Be Slow, Indecisive and Slightly Irrational. It always used to astonish me that relatively stupid people make deals where the bright and sparkling were failing. Yet it is something which one sees repeatedly.

The reason, I now believe, is that buyers are frightened by the brilliant sales presentation. Its power tends to overwhelm them.

By contrast, the quiet salesman is not a threat. He leaves the buyer feeling powerful. And if the quiet salesman is also a good listener, he can tailor his offer to fit closer to the Other Party. Add a quota of "Yes and . . ." comments, and the slow indecisive person is seen as an ally, different to the more sparkling and threatening competitor.

Set up a Study Group. When you are the boss and things are getting tough, send your production man off with his production man to thrash out the production aspects. Your finance man with his finance man. And so on. You will find that you and the other boss can enjoy yourselves with a game of golf while others thrash out the matter and you will make better progress in the relaxed atmosphere of the golf course, than in the taut atmosphere that had developed in the negotiating room.

And so we can go on. Tactics galore to suit the appetite of the healthiest of competitive negotiators.

And remember the two devices mentioned in Chapter 13; universally positive tactics:

> the recess
> the golf club.

EXERCISES

1. What peripherals would you leave out of the discussion on selling a motor car (Chapter 15) to be decided after you have wrung out the last half penny on price? (a) as seller, (b) as buyer.
2. What tactics would you plan to use as seller?

FURTHER READING

Video Arts (1985) *So You Think You Can Sell?* London: Methuen.
I am entirely in agreement with Bill Scott when he says that lack of authority should not be used as a tactic in negotiation. The Video Arts team suggest that the tactic should only be used to introduce a counter proposal of one's own, such as: "I could go back to Head Office, but I know they'd turn it down. *Now what if we . . .*". They also warn against tactics from the other side which may stampede an inexperienced negotiator into going beyond his authority, and conceding too much.

March, P.D.V. (1984) *Contract Negotiation Handbook.* Epping: Gower Press (2nd edn).
Treats the "straw man" issue as one of a set of defensive situational tactics. Marsh also gives a very revealing treatment of some of the difficulties of negotiating in other countries.

Walton, R.E. & McKersie, R.B. (1965) *A Behavioral Theory of Labor Negotiations.* New York: McGraw-Hill.
Walton & McKersie discuss the use of a number of tactics to record and analyse verbal and non-verbal reactions. Some of this analysis is quite useful but what is recommended has to be kept within the bounds of the possible. And what is possible is very much a function of negotiators' limited capacities to do two or more things at once. Remember, it is for this reason that Bill Scott introduced a number of devices to simplify negotiations and to guide drills.Thus, if you want to observe the reactions of the other team in some detail maybe you should ask a member of your team, not involved in the negotiations, to act as an observer. Walton & McKersie report that this is exactly what some firms do.

Karrass, G. (1985). *Negotiate to Close.* London: Fontana.
To say that this price is not negotiable does not exclude negotiation on other issues. This point is developed very well by Karrass and a number of other authors. To quote Karrass. "Even when dealing in fixed-price products, we negotiate. We negotiate terms, or delivery, or freight cost, or installation, or tie-in advertisements, or any one of many other things involved in many negotiations" (p. 140).

Scott, W.P. (1981) *The Skills of Negotiating.* Aldershot: Gower.
Outlines and discusses a number of competitive tactics with practical examples.

Karrass, C.L. (1974) *Give and Take.* World Book Co.
An extensive and often witty treatment of many negotiating tactics, both scrupulous and unscrupulous.

Nirenberg, GI. & Colero, H.H. (1971) *How to Read a Person Like a Book.* Hawthorne.
Many insights into expert views on body language.

CHAPTER 19
Settling

INTRODUCTION

Before tackling preparation for competitive negotiations and before further words on Planning and Control, this chapter completes the treatment of the subject matter.

This chapter is on the subject of Settling. It is a short chapter because it is a short phase. Short and time is critical.

It is all too easy to go wrong.

EXAMPLES

"Well," said Martin. "We have just about come to an agreement on this."

"Yes," said Guy. "All very good. I am very pleased."

"We had better just decide what to do about the colours."

Three hours later they were still at it. They were arguing about colours and shades, and there had crept in new issues about the price for shade variations and the effect that this would have on delivery.

They never settled the deal.

"Yes," said Howard. "We seem to be just about there. I am quite prepared to agree on this if you will increase the price by 1p."

"Not a hope, not a hope. A ½p is the furthest I can go," replied Lew.

"Well, if you are going to twist my tail on that, I suppose I shall have to accept just a ½p."

"Let's shake on that, and then we can get Harry and Geoff to sort out the colour."

COMMENTS

As negotiators sense the end of the negotiation there is an immediate increase in energy and activity. All of a sudden, after a long period of slow progress, the end is in sight. Shoulders go up, the beginnings of smiles appear. There is great promise.

But this promise is very short-lived. If you have been in a 3-week negotiation then it is the last evening and the morning of the final day. If you have been in a 2-hour negotiation, then it is the final 10 minutes.

No longer.

The new burst of energy is always short-lived and you exceed that short period at your peril.

It is all too easy to exceed it. The less experienced negotiators in this example, sensing the end in sight, try to use this promising period to sort out the detail of colour. They fail to seize the moment and the deal escapes from them.

The experienced negotiators, by contrast, seized the available agreement and agreed that subordinates should later sort out the detail of colour. They also successfully traded *the last half penny*. Any negotiator hopes to have achieved the best possible deal. If he leaves with the sense that maybe, with just a little more effort, he could have got a little more, then he goes away unsatisfied. Give him the satisfaction: make sure he appreciates that last half penny just as Lew and Howard gave each other that satisfaction.

Having given the satisfaction, quickly make use of the brief spurt of energy.

> Seize the available agreement.
> Summarize what has been agreed.
> Define the action and a schedule.

Other people can follow up on matters of detail. Go away with the available agreement.

SUMMARY

1. As a settlement nears, timing is of the essence.
2. Ask for the last half penny.
3. Seize the *available* agreement.
4. Summarize the agreement.
5. Define action.
6. Go.

FURTHER READING

There are three points here which are very important.

The first is that it is easy to miss an available agreement by getting bogged down in detail, or arguing about costs which are quite unimportant in the long run. A number of training exercises in negotiation are designed to make just this point. One example is:

Bass, B.M., Vaughan, J.A. & Cox, C. (1968) English version of Bass, B.M. (1967) Exercise Negotiations: Exercise 9 in *A Programme of Exercises for Management and Organizational Psychology*. European Research Group on Management (ERGOM), Vaarstraat 22/4B, Louvain, Belgium.

The second point is that someone has to follow up on the details. This won't happen. It has to be arranged.

The third point is that you have to wait until the right kind of agreement is available. Thus, Rackham & Morgan have pointed out that skilled negotiators are more willing to disagree in the final stages of negotiation than unskilled negotiators. They are not so concerned with reaching an agreement that almost any agreement will do. This point is amplified in:

Rackham, N. & Carlisle, J. (1978) The Effective Negotiator—Part 1. The Behaviour of Successful Negotiators. *Journal of European Industrial Training* **2** (6) 6–10.

Morley, I.E. (1981) Negotiation and Bargaining. In Argyle, M. (ed.) *Social Skills and Work*. London: Methuen.

CHAPTER 20

Preparation for Competitive Negotiations

INTRODUCTION

We considered in Chapters 9–11 preparation for Constructive Negotiation.

In this chapter we will first remind you of the major points previously made about preparation and will then make further points about

Preparation for different phases

Risks in preparation.

SUMMARY OF PREVIOUS POINTS

Preparation is a most important preliminary to negotiations. It readies the mind. It helps to minimize the overload which any negotiator will experience during the negotiation and it has a key effect in orienting the way negotiations will develop.

We have suggested that the outcome of a preparation process should be something very simple. The idea of four key words.

To reach that simplicity, we offered the A4/A5/A6 approach. First, brainstorm random ideas; second, analyse under four headlines and, finally, reduce each headline to one key word.

We also suggested three variations of this A6. First, the proposed procedure (Purpose, Plan and Pace); second, the intended output (the statement we will offer) and finally, the desired input (the questions which we hope the Other Party will tell us answers to).

For a constructive negotiation concentrating on the phase of Exploration, we suggest a very general sort of preparation, a general opening statement, plus some general questions designed to lead to a dialogue on creative possibilities and to recognizing shared goals.

PREPARATION FOR DIFFERENT PHASES

Whatever the phase you are entering in a negotiation, you need your mind prepared for the three different aspects:

To handle the procedure.
To make your presentation.
To act as a good listener.

You need also (it cannot be over-stressed) to have done your technical homework, to have researched your product, your specification, your offer, whatever may be the subject matter you will be dealing with.

You need also to have distinctive forms of preparation for:

Your strategy.
Exploration.
Bidding.
Bargaining.

Preparation of strategy

First, analyse the situation. Marsh (1984) deals handsomely with this phase of preparation. He particularly recommends consideration of the respective strengths of the two parties and of the likelihood of continued relationships.

If you are the only buyer and there are many competitors, then you should go for the Quick Kill.

You invite tenders to meet your needs. If, on the other hand, you are one of many competitors, then you are more likely to hold back.

For a major negotiation, analyse your strength and your vulnerabilities. Analyse also the strengths and the likely strategy of your competitors.

Gather information about the Other Party and analyse how they are likely to behave.

From this evidence, prepare your strategy and decide the style in which you will negotiate. If you find a competitive style to be appropriate, review the tactics you can use to gain the highest advantage for yourself. Review your agency agreement and particularly the support you will need from your agents if you are operating in some export markets.

This strategic preparation can be heavy in its time demands. It is necessary for major negotiations.

Preparation for exploration

Chapter 11 dealt with preparation for the exploration phase; it was taken as the key phase of a constructive negotiation. This preparation should be sufficiently general to lead to a dialogue on creative possibilities, but not so detailed that one's mind becomes inflexible.

Examples of the A6s for this phase were given in Figures 10.3, 11.1 and 11.2.

Preparation for bidding

In a competitive negotiation, if there has first been a phase of exploration, it is vital that the negotiator then takes fresh stock. He needs to take a break and to prepare afresh for the bargaining. He should take stock of the shape of the deal as it has emerged in discussion so far and consider the evidence he has about the prospective behaviour of the other party from now on.

If he is tendering, or if he is placing a bid which will be compared to competitors, then his guidance (from the sales side) is as before: make the Highest Defensible Bid.

That which is defensible in this case, is that which will ensure that one is invited to the next round of negotiations.

Bids must be worked out for each aspect of the deal which could be open to negotiations.

For a commercial deal—Price, Quality, Delivery, Settlement terms, Building terms, Performance, Guarantee, Cancellation costs, Penalties, a host of individual conditions for that special contract.

For an export credit—Political risk, Commercial risk, Total amount, Maximum stake, Rate.

Preparation of procedure and of one's own statement for this phase are obvious and the results are exemplified in Figures 20.1 and 20.2.

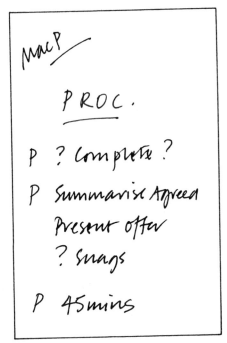

Fig. 20.1   A procedural A6 for the Bidding phase

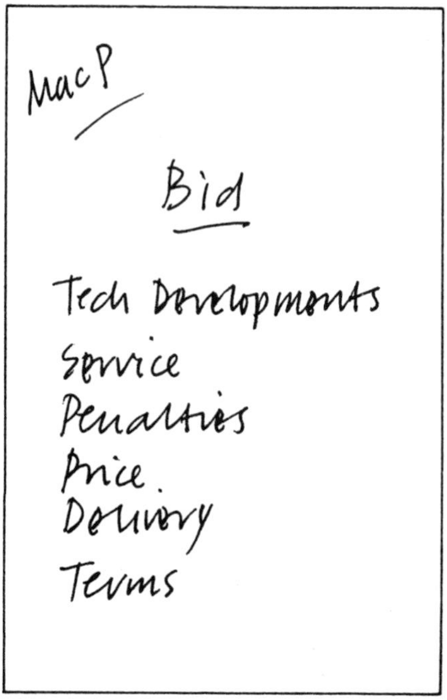

Fig. 20.2 Headlines for Bidding

Preparation for the listening aspect is less obvious.

The problem here is that one is going to have one's energy centred on putting one's bid. But once that bid has been put, it is important to switch wavelengths quickly. The other party is likely to try to chip away at one's bid and to leave one with a sense of the bid not being good enough, uncertain as to what aspects are not good enough or by how much. One then goes into the Bargaining phase confused, inadequately informed to handle that phase effectively, forced towards a demoralizing series of concessions without counter-trade.

"Well, there we are", said Howard. "That is what we can offer you and we have, of course, done our best to ensure that the deal will suit your needs as we understand them."

"O.K.", said Lew. "I think I get the picture, but I'm afraid it is too steep for us. You are going to have to reduce a lot."

This is the moment when Howard needs to be able to switch wavelengths. He needs to have done his thinking in advance so that he is ready for this moment. If he is ill-prepared he will probably find himself trying to refute Lew's "have to reduce a lot". This can only lead to the next stage being one of confrontation and loss. Better prepared, Howard might try to develop the discussion somewhat like this:

Howard: "I'm sorry to hear that. We felt that we had put together a deal which would be very constructive. Can you tell me the snags you are seeing?"

Lew: "The price is way up, the delivery is too long and we need better terms."

Howard: "I see, price, delivery and terms. That's very tough. However, I think that our quality record speaks for itself and, of course, you know that we have never let you down on delivery. Your production people have been satisfied with the way we have trained their staff and you know the way our technical people get on with one another."

Lew: "Yes, I grant you that much but price, delivery and terms, you are way out there."

Howard: "Well I will certainly take another look to see if we can make any difference, but can you tell me where your priorities lie. I will move as far as I can but do you want me to place more emphasis on price than on delivery for example?"

Lew: "We must have both. The delivery date is quite fundamental and there is no hope unless you can match us on that."

Howard: "So that if I go away and take your delivery as essential and then look at the price in that context . . ."

Lew: "Yes, I suppose that is a good way of doing it, but you will have to get the price down too."

Howard: "If I worked on that, then would you be prepared to meet me on the terms?"

Lew: "Well not entirely, but if you can manage the delivery at a much better price, then it is worth discussing further."

Howard: "Thank you very much. Can you help me one stage further. Can you give me some indication of your thinking on the price issue?"

Lew: "Well, it is fair to say that we do have some people who are offering at 12 per cent less."

Howard: "Most helpful. Thank you very much, I will go away and see what we can do to meet your needs here.
"Will it be all right if I come again next Tuesday?"

For the third of his A6 notes, the information he needed from the buyer, Howard had written three words: Snags, Priorities, Indications (Fig. 20.3).

The skilled competitive negotiator prepares not only his plan and his own statements for the bidding phase, he prepares his mind to handle the other party's reponse.

He should emerge in a good position to prepare for the bargaining phase.

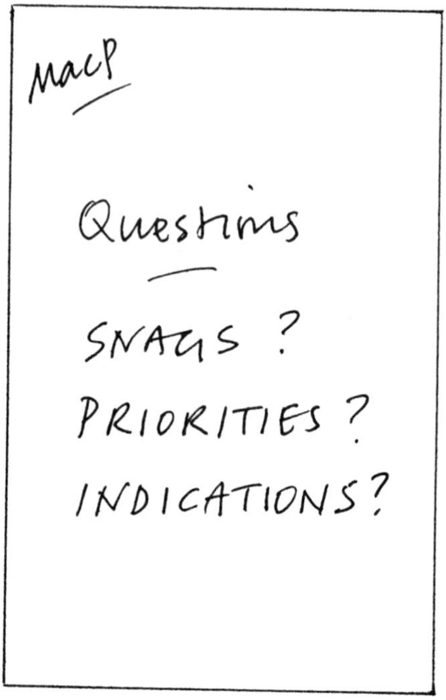

Fig. 20.3   A "questions" A6 for Bidding phase

Preparation for bargaining

Successful bargaining depends first on attitudes. It is important to be positive and creative, as opposed to negative and hostile. It is important to remember that with minimum prejudice to your own needs you should help him to take home a satisfying deal. Nevertheless, your prime responsibility is to represent your own side. You need your thinking clear for that responsibility.

Go through the full list of variables to be negotiated.
Define those on which you can make no concession.
Note the other party's priorities which you should have found out at the end of the bidding phase.
Prepare for the measured pace of a bargaining ritual; the size and timing of concessions you may have to make and of the counter-concessions you will require at the same time from the other party.

Figures 20.4 and 20.5 give examples of no concession lists and of measured paces.

Complement with another A6, equivalent to a questions A6, to

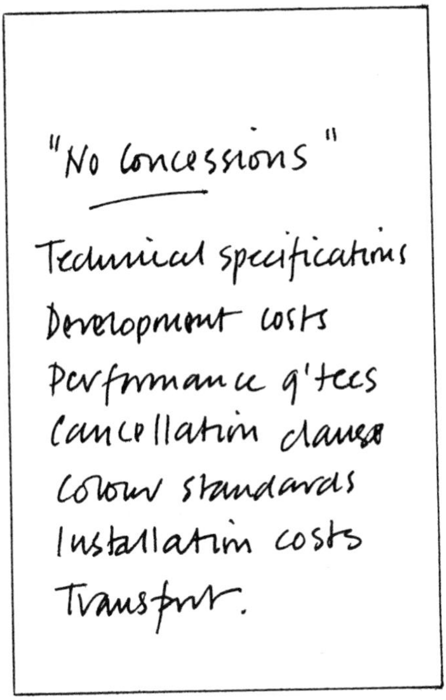
"No Concessions"

Technical specifications
Development costs
Performance g'tees
Cancellation clauses
Colour standards
Installation costs
Transport.

Fig. 20.4 No Concession list

prepare your thinking to be positive and supportive to the Other Party (Fig. 20.6)

RISKS IN PREPARATION

There are three main types of risk in preparation.

Under-doing preparation
The most frequent regret I hear from negotiators is "We were not well enough prepared". Generally I believe them. Negotiators are busy people and find it all too difficult to find the time to do their preparation adequately. Moreover, many lack the sort of discipline and a type of time-effective system such as this book has tried to suggest.

Over-doing preparation
I am not always convinced that the claim "not well enough prepared" is correct. It is impossible to anticipate and to be prepared for every eventuality. Some things are going to catch you unawares and you run risks if you do too much to pre-empt them.

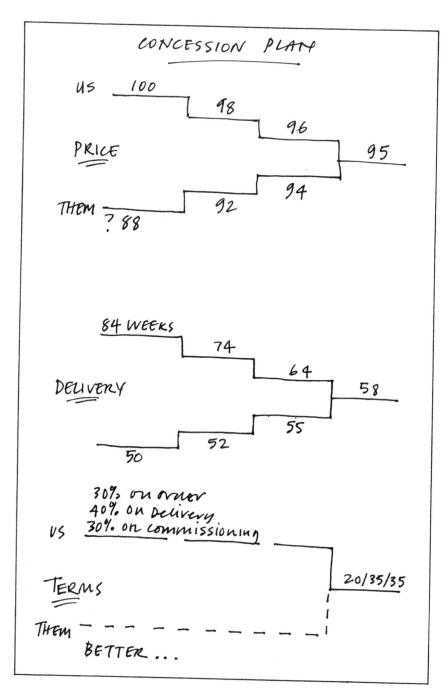

Fig. 20.5   Planned concessions

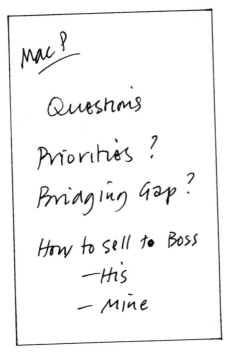

Fig. 20.6   Prepare to consider the other's interests

Premature preparation

If you have prepared hard for bidding and bargaining phases too soon, you will not be able to conduct a creative exploratory phase. Your mind will be fenced off from that creativity fenced into proffering your bids too quickly, pushing the other party into defensive responses.

He was an eminent Norwegian running his Company's extensive interests in the Far East.

At the outset of a Seminar he said to me "Bill, there is one thing that I want before I leave this Seminar—that is to know how on earth to handle the Koreans".

During the Seminar I invited him to conduct a synthetic "negotiation" with other delegates. I asked him to think of those other delegates as tough competitive people. I asked him at the outset to prepare the bids he would eventually make and be prepared for a tough bargaining phase. I asked him to think of the tactics he would use in that situation.

He did so excellently.

His later comment was "I am astonished. It was only an exercise but I was totally bound up in it. I found myself behaving exactly as the Koreans do when I try to negotiate with them. Quite astonishing".

It was an example of premature preparation.

SUMMARY

1. The start point for this chapter was that we have previously emphasized the importance of preparation, offered the process of the A4/A5/A6 approach and suggested its use for the exploration stage, the threefold use, procedure, statement and questions.

2. Strategic preparation:

   Assess your strengths and vulnerabilities
   Assess the competition
   Assess the other party
   Decide on your strategy

3. Preparation for Bidding:

   The highest defensible bid
   All variables identified
   Snags
   Priorities?
   Hints?

4. Preparation for bargaining:

   No concession list
   Pace of traded concessions.

5. Strike a balance between under-doing and over-doing preparation.

EXERCISE

1. You will be negotiating on behalf of a medical charity with a firm of property developers for the purchase of an old building which has been refurbished as a rest home or nursing home. The building was originally an 8-bedroom private house standing in ¾ acre of parkland/garden. It has been rebuilt to provide a large lounge, a dining room, 12 bedrooms, kitchens, 5 bathrooms and a 3-room staff flat. The grounds have been cleared of grass, plants and trees and the top soil sold off. All these rooms have light and curtain fittings and the floors are covered with vinyl tiles. The kitchen and bathrooms are basically equipped.

   The charity has substantial funds and is committed to acquiring a property in this area but obviously wants to buy as cheaply as possible. The developers have a reputation for being hard, even unscrupulous, negotiators with no record of making any concessions for charities.

   The asking price quote by their agent is £275,000 which seems excessive when local hearsay is that they bought the site for £60,000 and in addition to the top soil, sold off many antique and Victorian fittings.

Prepare for the negotiation.

FURTHER READING

Atkinson, G.G.M. (1975) *The Effective Negotiator* London: Quest
Atkinson deals explicitly with preparation for competitive negotiations which he calls distributive bargaining. The major elements of preparation are introduced under the headings of bargaining power; conventions of bargaining; strategies of bargaining; and the case, the agenda and the bargaining team.

Morley, I.E. (1982) Preparation for Negotiation. In Bradstatter, H., Davis, J.H. & Stocker-Kreichgauer, G. (eds) *Group Decision Making*. London: Academic Press.
This is advanced reading in general. However, part of the paper deals with the negotiations at the Paris Peace Conference of 1919 which led to the Treaty of Versailles. The American negotiating team were so badly prepared that they were always working within frameworks defined by the British or the French. This meant that they were almost always seen as obstructive and ignorant. The negotiations have not been judged a success.

Rackham, N. & Carlisle, J. (1978)The Effective Negotiator—Part 2. Planning for Negotiations. *Journal of European Industrial Training* 2 (7) 2–5.
Identifies some of the risks of overdoing preparation and shows some of the ways in which skilled negotiators avoid them.

Marsh, P.D.V. (1984) *Contract Negotiating Handbook*. Aldershot: Gower.
Analyses strategic planning for negotiations with special references to power positions.

CHAPTER 21
Planning and Control

INTRODUCTION

In any form of negotiation, procedural Planning and Control should be highly influential.

The points made about these topics in Part 1 remain the valid points.

EXAMPLES

Arnold is a paper merchant dealing in very large quantities. He was in search of a new source of base paper, to be coated for a new end use.

There were two likely sources of supply, one in England and one in Sweden. He first flew to Stockholm to explore the specifications and to negotiate terms.

After about 10 minutes there arose the question as to whether the deal should be made in pounds sterling or in kroner. This led to a prolonged discussion on exchange rates. How they had fluctuated, how they were likely to fluctuate and the steps to be taken if they did fluctuate.

It was a very prolonged discussion and Arnold was left with little time at the end of it to discuss specifications or to negotiate terms.

Those items, the main purpose for his visit, had to be concentrated into the last 15 minutes or so when he should have been in a taxi taking him back to the airport. The key items were skimped and had to be elaborated in lengthy telephone calls and telexes.

All very unsatisfactory. The negotiations had been a waste of time.

Arnold next visited the English company and told them of how he had been to Sweden and been trapped in the discussion of exchange rates. The Sales Director, whom he was meeting, was immediately full of interest. "Ah now, that's just the sort of problem we face in getting our pulp from Canada. What solution did you find?"

And so Arnold told him about the discussion in Stockholm. And now the discussion in England began to cover exchange rate variations for the imported pulp and how those variations should be resolved for the paper for Arnold's special requirements.

*Once again the negotiating time was commandeered by the discussion of
exchange rates. The negotiations were again largely a waste of time, again
because of the lack of planning and control.*

Let's imagine how Lew might have acted if he had been in the same
position.

Lew flew out to Stockholm and in the plane he read again the
specification and noted the more difficult points in it. He reviewed his
thoughts about procedure, both for the technical discussion and for the
commercial discussion.

On arrival, and after the opening formalities, he sat down and said
"Well now, I am glad to be here and hope during today to be able to have
a full discussion about technical needs, and also to arrive at an
understanding of the commercial possibilities. Would it be in order for
me to suggest that we concentrate this morning on the technical matters
and take this afternoon on the commercial?"

Quickly he was in the Technical Director's office. He had previously
sent a copy of his specification and he now asked his hosts first to present
their overall comment on the specification and then that they should go
through it item by item.

Being Lew, and being accustomed to keeping control of negotiations,
he made a point of checking progress every 20 minutes or so, checking
that his hosts were satisfied that they were moving at a speed to finish the
technical discussions during the morning. It would not be an easy
discussion but it would be a productive one.

After lunch and the opening formalities of the afternoon session, Lew
opened:

"Well, gentlemen, thank you very much for your hospitality today. I
would like to leave here with firm offers to meet our needs and I have to
be on the 16.35 plane. Do think it would be possible within that time?

"May I suggest how we tackle this afternoon's discussion?

"I would be grateful if you could give me a comprehensive offer to start
with. Then possibly we could go through it item by item.

"The items which I expect to need discussion are:

> Price
> Delivery
> Settlement Terms
> Quality Guarantee
> Exchange Rates
> Default Arrangements

"Would that be a satisfactory way of tackling it for you?"
*With his developed knack of checking progress and keeping negotiations
to a realistic time schedule, Lew would be able to sustain that progress, to
keep to his plan and to the schedule.*

141

The first pair of examples are from real life. They show negotiations frustrated by inadequate Planning and Control.

The second example is an imaginary one of a negotiator making the most of his negotiating opportunities. In his preparation for the negotiation he thought through the procedure he would try to adopt. He cleared his mind about the purpose of his visit, the form the agenda should take and the time available for discussion.

He put these thoughts to his hosts and achieved their agreement to his plan.

He had also developed the skill of periodically breaking out of discussing details of the subject, to keep progress under control.

Consequences: efficient and effective negotiations.

SUMMARY

1. Plan the way you intend a negotiation to develop.
2. Regularly check progress in relation to that plan.
3. Keep time under control.

EXERCISES

1. Based on the preparation carried out in the exercise in Chapter 20, build a plan to put forward to the developer's negotiator, with a time schedule.
2. Form two groups, each of two members. If numbers are available also have two observers.

   Group A has as its brief the information at the end of Chapter 20.

   Group B's brief is as follows. You are the property developers negotiating to sell the refurbished property. You actually bought the site for £75,000 and realized £60,000 from the sale of the top soil and various antique fittings. Using your own labour and equipment the cost of refurbishing was £80,000 after allowing a reasonable amount for overheads. You are asking £275,000 for the property but, because of cash-flow problems in the firm, you have been given permission to negotiate around this figure.

   The two parties should spend about 20 minutes discussing their strategy and plans and 30 minutes in negotiation. The observers should be present during the planning stage, sit in on the negotiations and then report back

   (a) whether or not their team achieved its objectives,
   (b) what the obstacles were to agreement and how they were overcome.

FURTHER READING

Carlisle, J. (1981) Negotiating Groups. In Payne, R. & Cooper, C. (eds) *Groups at Work*. Chichester: Wiley.
Carlisle discusses a number of ways in which negotiations might develop. He attempts to show some of the ways in which effective negotiators control the pace of negotiations, and keep them on an appropriate track.

Scott, W. (1981) *The Skills of Negotiating*. Aldershot: Gower.
Provides further examples of some of the points made in this chapter.

CHAPTER 22
Team Negotiations

INTRODUCTION

So far we have been assuming that a negotiator is operating on his own. The position becomes more complicated when there is a team of negotiators and particularly when that team is to negotiate over a long period.

In this chapter we shall be looking at Team Negotiations under the headings.

> Team selection
> Team formation
> Team preparation

TEAM SELECTION

There are many negotiations in which more expertise is needed than one negotiator can offer. So the negotiation team becomes two colleagues. It may even need to become more.

If you are negotiating a complicated deal in China, then you need not only a commercial negotiator but a technical expert, a financial expert, somebody knowledgeable in counter trade, and you are likely to need experts to look after the training of the local staff and half a dozen other matters. This introduces too large a number to form a comfortable team.

There is a limit to the number of people who can participate effectively at any one time.

In my view, that maximum is four. That is the maximum number who can concentrate and contribute in one session.

If more people need to be present to know what is going on, by all means have them along, but seated behind the negotiators and not at the negotiating table.

By all means change the constitution of the four front row people. Let them change chairs, preferably between sessions and not during them.

Additional expertise is not the only reason for sometimes increasing the size of a negotiating group.

If you go to Cuba or China, or indeed most Communist countries, you will find yourself faced with possibly ten other people on the opposite side of a large table. For the individual negotiator on his own this can be demoralizing. He needs a supporter for the sake of morale, even if not for added expertise.

You need to take account of the people with whom you are going to negotiate.

One aspect is the culture of the Other Party, a subject which we shall tackle in more detail during the next chapter. But in matters of team selection, if you are going to Germany with its high regard for formality and authority, then there is a need to take people with high formal qualifications. If you are going to China and many other Eastern countries, then the team must include delegates of impressive status. The significance of this status is such that at least one of my distinguished clients has given the title of Vice-President to every member of their marketing staff.

There are experts who believe that a negotiating team ought to operate as a democratic grouping with the team leader acting as a coordinator, rather than as a spokesman. I do not always accept that view.

If all members of a team are accustomed to working in an autocratic environment, then they will be at their best when working in an autocratically led team.

I know of team leaders who act as sole spokesman for their teams. If they need information which they do not have themselves, they turn to a colleague. They ask him for that information. They then themselves present the information across the table to the Other Party.

It is highly dictatorial but it is what the team members are accustomed to. It is the way in which that team is at its most effective.

This is by no means to suggest that all teams should work in that sort of way. It is comparatively rare for organizations to operate in such a dictatorial way and it should be only the teams from such organizations who use that style.

There is a wide variety of different styles, from the dictatorial through the formal and the informal to differing degrees of democracy.

At the far extreme, it is possible to have a leader who sees his role as concentrating on planning and control. He delegates to members of his team the responsibility for all negotiations within their own specialisms.

It is tempting to think that such a leader can stay calmly above the "hurly-burly" which is likely to develop all around him. It is tempting, but few of us have the capacity to resist jumping in, in support of our people, when the going gets tough.

Nevertheless, if a leader manages to do so, he can control both the development of the current meeting and the strategic development of the full negotiation. Such a leader, for example, is well positioned when knotty issues are proving difficult, to propose that they be delegated to task groups from the two parties. He will also be well positioned to form an alliance with the Other Party's team leader—a much easier alliance than the protagonist can form.

Teams will always be forced to some extent to accommodate to the Other Party's style of operating. Nevertheless, the basic advice is simple: try to operate in your normal style. The one that you can adopt without having to think about it while there are so many other demands on your energies.

TEAM FORMATION

In this section we shall assume that a team is being formed to conduct a negotiation of great significance, one which is expected to be lengthy.
  Once a team has been chosen, it needs to build up teamwork.
  Go off to the country for a teamwork weekend. In this period, work through the team's aspirations. Have each member present state his hopes and his fears for the negotiation. Let this discussion build into an agenda to be reviewed during the weekend. Expect it to raise major issues which will confront the team during the negotiation. Have each issue studied and decide on action needed to prepare for that issue.
  If possible, bring in members of the back-up team; those whose support from back home will be essential whilst the team is out in the field. This team-building is so important that it is worth getting an expert in team-building to mastermind the weekend for the team.
  Ensure that the discussion includes the communication processes that will be needed between negotiators and back-up. Avoid leaving it to chance, "We will ring when there is anything to talk about". Make specific arrangements. For example, full reports every Saturday on the week's progress; re-appraisal of objectives and of targets for next week.

PREPARATION

All team members need to be involved in the preparation. There are going to be heavy stresses on their cooperation when the negotiation gets started. The understanding established between them in the preparation phase can stave off later crises in cooperation.
  Once the team has been formed and started working as a team, the next stage is technical preparation. Ensure that the subject matter is

thoroughly researched and that suitable presentations and visual displays are prepared.

At the same time, do your homework on the Other Party. Think of the style in which they are likely to negotiate. Find out all you can about the individuals you are likely to meet and again think of the way in which they will negotiate. Now draw your team together and thrash out your strategy. If at all possible, include the home-based back-up teams again.

Agree roles and responsibilities.

If it is Chris's job to handle the commercial aspects, Frank's the financial and Ted's the technical, then make sure that each is quite clear about his responsibilities. Do ensure that Chris is not going to try to lead in the discussion on quality (that's Ted's task) nor in discussing the way the deal will be financed (that's up to Frank). Make sure too that neither Frank nor Ted will involve himself in the bargaining on commercial matters.

All too often one sees the technical expert jumping into the commercial arena and yielding ground for which the commercial man has fought very hard. If you are going to have a four-man team, here is one hint which is found to be invaluable by experienced negotiators.

Appoint one member of the team to take responsibility for procedure. One member who will be in charge of the planning and control foundation. He does not have to be the team leader. Indeed, many team leaders become so captivated in the content of the negotiation that they lose the ability to sit back and calmly keep an eye on how things are developing.

These can be great men who may never realize until somebody else points it out, that they are spending hours splitting hairs. Such people have the capacity to accept the need for planning and control and then to take pride in being controlled by their own subordinates.

Once the overall preparation is complete, begin to think about the way you will handle each session. As ever, there is the need to think it through to the simplicity of three A6 sheets. There is a need to reconcile different views within a team and to take them through to unanimity. It is no use a team going into a negotiation with half-baked ideas, or without mutual commitment.

For a negotiation of major significance, rehearse your presentation and, using colleagues role-playing the other party, rehearse major negotiating sessions.

SUMMARY

1. Keep the team small, no more than four members at the table.
2. Start with a teamwork weekend.

3. Involve the back-up team.
4. Prepare fully as a team.

EXERCISE

1. In the examples of negotiating the football team transport (Chapter 1), the Students' Union bar decoration (Chapter 3) and the project negotiation (Chapter 6), how would your negotiating teams have been constituted?

FURTHER READING

Marsh, P.D.V. (1984) *Contract Negotiating Handbook*. Epping: Gower Press. (2nd edn).
   The special problems of negotiating in teams have been largely ignored in the literature on the negotiation. Peter Marsh is one of the few writers who has taken them seriously. His discussion of the skills required by the team leader is highly recommended.

Scott W. (1981) *The Skills of Negotiating*. Aldershot: Gower.
   Bill Scott has discussed the importance of teamwork and identified some of the important elements in his previous book. Although the general treatment is much the same as that given here, the earlier work provides a number of further examples, based on Bill's practical experience.

Belbin, R.M. (1981) *Management Teams: Why They Succeed or Fail*. London: Heinemann.
   This is not a book about negotiation. But it is a good book about various kinds of management teams. Belbin identifies eight jobs (or roles) that have to be carried out within a decision making group. They cannot all be done by one person, and some of the roles are easier to combine than others. Belbin argues that decision-making is likely to go wrong unless sufficient attention is paid to each of the roles. Some of the examples Bill Scott has given would be very easy to translate into Belbin's frame of reference and his book is well worth reading.

CHAPTER 23

Negotiating Cultures

INTRODUCTION

Each of us has his own style of operating. His own style of negotiating.

Each of us is most effective when operating in a style that suits his own personality. If you are naturally a person who lives in an authoritative environment, if you jump to attention when the boss passes by and if you expect your subordinates to do the same when you pass them, then you will be most effective if you negotiate in a correspondingly dictatorial way. On the other hand, if you are at your best in a more democratic society, then you will be best in a more democratic style of negotiation

There are great differences in the way in which people negotiate from one country to another. I do not recommend that you should try to negotiate in the style which people use in such different countries: you are good at your way of operating and it is impossible for you to operate as well in a radically different style.

You will nevertheless be exposed to negotiators who operate very differently. You will find many shocks. You will have to tolerate and even be responsive to such shocking behaviour.

This chapter is about some of the differences which you can anticipate as you move from one culture to another. It is a chapter distilled from the wisdom of many negotiators who have suffered the shocks. People who have been confronted with ways of negotiating which they find totally different to their normal style. The author has himself been involved in negotiating with most of these cultures but at the outset acknowledges his indebtedness to those with richer experience.

The Northern European culture is highly constructive. The Scandinavian in particular, the British to a lesser extent, have a great capacity for open, honest, creative negotiation. They are stubborn people and once they have specified their position openly, honestly, they stick tenaciously to that position.

"Well, all right I understand you. But I have told you my needs. How would that help me?"

These characteristics make them natural masters of the constructive style of negotiating. They are expert at stating their needs, reasonably good at listening to other people's positions and highly interested in a

149

creative search for opportunities. They are relatively low in their ability to break the ice and they do not find the wheeling and dealing of bargaining to be easy.

We British have the reputation of being

Heavy lunchers
Amateurs
Dislikers of bad news
Ritual dressers

We have a reputation for opening the negotiations with a heavy lunch. It embarrasses our visitors who take light lunches and do not have any gins and tonics before the evening.

We are seen to be amateurs. Not any ordinary amateurs but very professional ones. We are seen to make a point of not knowing all the details which an American or a German would know. We are seen to be distasteful of such professionalism.

"Ah, yes, the colour range. Afraid that I am not too strong on that. You don't mind if I ring somebody else about that, do you?"

Contrast the American comment in the same situation.

"The colour range? Sure, we can meet you totally on colour ranges. We have experts here who have worked on that over the past 17 years. I can even get hold of one of them here and now if you like. Would you like that?"

We British are also seen to be people who do not like to give bad news. Consider the following dialogue.

Seller: "We can offer delivery in 9 months."
Buyer: "That will not do. We need it in 3 months."
Seller: "Oh, that is difficult. Our present deliveries are 9 months but if it is important for you to have it sooner we will do our best."

The customer at this point is likely to hear "We will do our utmost to deliver in 3 months. Don't worry about it."

The British seller on the other hand is really saying that 3 months is impossible. He means something like "I will do my best to do it in 9 months or even less and not let it drag on for 12 months." This veiled reluctance to give bad news has confused many of our international customers.

We are seen to be a little eccentric about our clothing. There is a need to wear formal dress which is no longer the custom elsewhere. I share this view. I have several immaculate suits and always wear one of them when doing business in England. But abroad a sports jacket and slacks or practical clothing are the accepted fashion in most countries outside the EEC.

Elsewhere in the EEC clothing tends to be equally formal but there are other variations of negotiating cultures.

The Germans, more specifically the North Germans, are brilliant at preparing for negotiations. They go into enormous depth. They think out their propositions in great detail and present them authoritatively and conscientiously.

This detailed preparation means that they are low in versatility during negotiations. Equally, their follow-up is brilliant as long as they can stick to their highly developed plans. Less effective if there are snags in implementing the plans.

My golf partner is Production Director of a company manufacturing household furniture. Once, the golf round was enlivened by his story of recent negotiations with a German Machinery supplier.

"Everything is worked out down to the last detail. They have even told us that we have to close the factory for 2 weeks whilst they move everything. They have specified the particular weeks and we are going to arrange that that will be the holiday period. It is planning such as none of our own companies could possibly manage."

Four months later, we were playing golf again. My friend had just started his holiday and was keeping well out of the way.

A week later I rang him for another game of golf and he was not available. The story came out a few weeks later.

"I went in to check how they were getting on and there was nobody there. There had been some snags about materials arriving—nobody had told us, and there has been chaos ever since."

This used to be a rare story. Generally the superb planning of the Germans pays off. But they are not so good when things go wrong.

If negotiating with Germans, be alive also to their commitment to formality and authority. You need to have with you experts with high technical qualifications.

In the States, we enter a different world of negotiating. Our first impression is of warmth and hospitality. We are soon introduced into a hospitable household, we meet the family and the kids, we feel very much at home.

Then next morning we meet our charming host in the negotiating room. Once again there is great warmth. But at the negotiating table we find a really tough negotiator. This is for him the natural way to carry out a negotiation. It is natural to try every technical trick. Wheeling and dealing and making fast bucks are the hallmarks of the high quality negotiator.

To the Briton, it is not the sort of thing which gentlemen would do. To our American friends that is how the cookie crumbles. That is what it is all about.

151

There is a great wealth of American literature on negotiating in this mould, see Further Reading.

In Japan, once again we enter into another negotiating world. The Japanese are quite incomprehensible to the Western mind. For example, the individual in Japan is of no significance, none whatsoever. What matters is the group. The tribe. The company. The Japanese espouse three main religions: Shintoism, Buddhism and Confucianism. To a Western mind these are three totally separate religions, each with its own ethics. Each radically different from the next. But to the Japanese there is no problem in espousing all three at one and the same time. Thus there is nothing confusing about having superb miniature ornamental gardens surrounded by massive ugly advertising hoardings. That is the meeting point of the three religions.

Confucianism lays heavy emphasis on status. Women are low in status and indeed only 20 years ago it was still the legal duty of the wife to pay her husband's brothel bills.

Such cultural difference from the European example spills over into the Negotiating Room. The brilliant Japanese negotiator is from a different culture from his European or American counterpart and his behaviour is naturally different. You will never understand it, but there are some ground rules.

One of them relates to time. You will need at least 3 times as long to negotiate a deal with the Japanese compared with someone from a Western culture. This is not because the Japanese are slow; it is because everyone in the group must be consulted before any deal can be agreed. This time element is very frustrating to Western negotiators, but once the deal is agreed, just watch the Japanese move. Everyone is committed, everyone is involved and their implementation is superb.

The word 'no' does not exist in their language. Questions which can be answered 'yes' or 'no' will always be answered 'yes'. In fact I am told that the word 'yes' in Japanese can be said in 20 different inflections to convey 20 or more different meanings. Such customs can easily mislead another negotiator, but recognize that it is a cultural difference, not a deliberate attempt to mislead. Indeed, the Japanese are reputed to take the view that "anybody who deliberately tries to mislead in a negotiation is a fool".

In most of the rest of the world there is another foundation level which you must respect before you can hope to do business. It is the foundation level of lubrication. You may think this sounds unethical, not the sort of thing that you and I would do or even know how to do. Quite right, but to the great majority of people in this world, there is no question about it. It is a way of life, and if you cannot cope with local customs, you do not deserve to do business.

I am not suggesting that you should go in for lubrication or bribery. For most Western people, it is illegal. It is equally immoral, and they are not competent in the art.

It is, nevertheless, a way of life on the majority of the world's surface and you will not do business unless you respect the way of life.

The way to do it is to appoint an agent of repute and to pay him the going rate of commission. It is then up to him to ensure that the local conditions are achieved and you should keep well out of the way.

It is imperative to take advice from knowledgeable people you can trust before appointing such an Agent. It is a key to your success in most parts of the world.

The Middle East presents a culture shock to the negotiator first going out there. The time dimension is protracted beyond all Western credibility. Go out tomorrow for an urgent meeting at their request and you will be lucky to get in to see anybody in less than 6 weeks.

Unless he is one of the increasing number of Harvard-trained negotiators, expect him to be sitting on a pedestal behind a massive desk, a long table stretching forward at ground level from that desk, 30 or 40 people around it and you somewhere at the bottom end. People constantly coming and going, haphazardly and inexplicably.

Muslims must from time to time go out to pray. Do not be surprised if your host suddenly goes outside to do so.

When you finally manage a quiet word with the great man, do not let it be on business, it will take you more weeks before you have acceptability to mention such delicate matters. So have your quiet word with the great man and do not be surprised when almost immediately his cousin takes his attention for some domestic matter.

Do respect his good intentions. He almost certainly has the best of intentions. If they do not come to fruition do not be frustrated. It is "Insah' Allah", the will of God.

The Far East does not have one negotiating culture but an infinity of cultures varying from one country to the next.

These differences are reflected in the minutest of details. For example, in Korea it is imperative to present your business card with ritual significance. You present it held in the thumb and forefinger of both hands with elaborate formality.

In Indonesia, the same practice would immediately disgrace you. The dominant religion in Indonesia is Muslim and the left hand is regarded as unclean.

Such details will influence one's ability to perform and it is imperative to have a detailed briefing on each specific country in the Far East.

Wherever you may be going, you will find negotiating has new dimensions. Ensure that you are briefed in detail on the local customs before you try to operate in a different culture.

FURTHER READING

Graham, J.L. & Sano, Y. (1986) *Smart Bargaining: Doing Business with the Japanese*. Cambridge, Mass.: Ballinger (2nd edn).
Now available in paperback and highly recommended by those with some experience of negotiating with the Japanese.

McCall, J.B. & Warrington, M.B. (1984) *Marketing by Agreement: A Cross-cultural Approach to Business Negotiations*. Chichester: Wiley.
McCall & Warrington provide some very useful case material, and provide a very wide ranging treatment of the problems of negotiating abroad. They point out the special importance of being patient in "high-context" cultures 'which place a high premium on personal relationships being the key to good business relationships" (p. 260).

Morley, I.E. & Stephenson, G.M. (1977) *The Social Psychology of Bargaining*. London: George Allen & Unwin.
A number of experimental studies suggest that cooperation and competition may be defined in different ways in different countries. A short review of this literature is given on pp. 79–81.

CHAPTER 24
Conclusion

INTRODUCTION

This final chapter begins with a reiteration of three of the concepts which have been underlying the treatment of negotiating. It concludes with a reminder of the framework, and of its distinctive applications to constructive and to competitive negotiations.

The three underlying concepts are

> overload
> ambiguity
> expectation.

OVERLOAD

The human mind is very good at dealing with a range of impulses but it can be overloaded by the weight and wealth of impressions coming to the mind during a negotiation, combined with the need to think about those impressions and to react to them, the need to articulate one's own position, the weight of what one is going to say next. It is too much to cope with effectively.

Throughout the book we have been emphasizing three steps to minimize that overload:

1. Forming an understanding of the process of negotiating and attempting to control within distinguishable phases.
2. Preparation to ensure clarity at the back of one's mind.
3. Drills: disciplines that one uses repeatedly and automatically without having to place a burden on the mind.

AMBIGUITY

The human mind is good at coping with difficult issues which it can recognize. It is ineffective when meandering around in an ill-defined environment. There is bound to be ambiguity in any negotiation. You are bound to find that there are some aspects of the Other Party's needs or thoughts which you cannot wholly understand, let alone accept. Nevertheless you have to do business under those conditions.

155

To minimize the problem of ambiguity we have recommended three forms of practice:

1. Clarify the procedure. Do not let that be an added burden during your negotiations.
2. Explore the negotiating ground with the Other Party. Get the best possible understanding of his position and adjust yours with him to create mutual advantage and to reduce ambiguity.
3. Try to avoid ambiguity during the bargaining phase. Work hard for counter-offers or at least for hints and indications.

EXPECTATIONS

Expectations are now recognized to be highly important in the field of motivation. The skilled negotiator is aware that he is constantly creating such important expectations.

Expectations of:

1. Procedure: the way in which the negotiation will unfold and the pace at which it will move.
2. Shared goals: expectations reached early in the negotiation about the way in which it should prove to be of benefit to both parties.
3. Bidding: expectations of the level at which a settlement might be achieved.
4. In the bargaining phase, positive expectations. The underlying theme that "this is a gap we must close" rather than "there is a massive gulf between us."

These are brief statements of underlying themes. They will be treated at greater length in a successor book.

SUMMARY

This book is focused on a framework to unravel the mysteries of negotiations.

It has been in two main parts.

The first part concentrated on constructive negotiations, the ways in which the attitudes of negotiators are constructive: open, honest, focused on the achievement of positive business relationships. A style of negotiating to mutual satisfaction, mutual profit.

The second part of the book encompassed the attitudes of competitive negotiators. A style in which each negotiator is concerned more with his own advantage than with mutual advantage. A style in which some degree of openness and honesty may yield to the supposed advantage of a measure of bluff and of technical ploys.

Throughout the book, we have used a consistent framework. In advance of the negotiations there is a need to have one's mind prepared, to have it as ready as possible to cope with the extreme load to which it will be subjected. We have offered the A4/A5/A6 technique as an aid to preparing the mind. Whether or not that process suits you, we still advocate the end product: the simplicity of four key words.

That preparation we have stressed in a particular form for the exploration phase—the key phase of a constructive negotiation.

We have suggested alternative ways for preparing a strategy and in advance of the bidding phase and of the bargaining phase.

We have emphasized the importance of building a suitable climate for negotiation. Cordial, cooperative, brisk and businesslike.

We have underlined the importance of procedure in negotiations. The early need to establish. Purpose, Plan and Pace. The continuing need to take stock of progress and time.

The subject matter we have broken down into four elements of EBBS:

Exploration: to establish one another's perspective and to build common goals.

Bidding: the highest defensible bid, presented unequivocally.

Bargaining: a positive stage of trading concessions and moving at a measured pace towards achieving a mutually satisfying deal.

Settling: a final short phase in which time is of the essence.

The whole is summarized in Fig. 24.1.

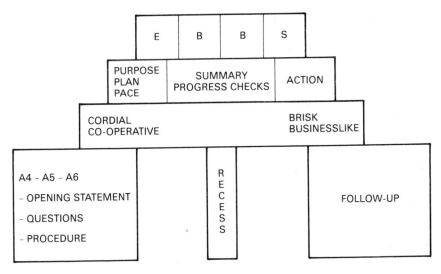

Fig. 24.1

Index